THE ULTIMATE CHINESE COOKBOOK FOR BEGINNERS

Unlock the Hidden Gems of Chinese Culinary Traditions and Immerse Yourself in a World of Exquisite Flavors and Endless Inspiration

Chu Hua

TABLE OF CONTENTS

CHAPTER 1: UNDERSTANDING CHINESE CUISINE 13

1.1 INTRODUCTION TO CHINESE CUISINE 13

    1.1.1 History and Influences 14

    1.1.2 Regional Varieties 15

1.2 EXPLORING CANTONESE CUISINE 16

    1.2.1 Characteristics and Flavors 16

    1.2.2 Popular Cantonese Dishes 17

1.3 CONTRASTING CHINESE AND CANTONESE COOKING 18

    1.3.1 Ingredients and Flavor Profiles 19

    1.3.2 Cooking Techniques and Traditions 20

CHAPTER 2: CHINESE CULINARY TRADITIONS 23

2.1 FESTIVALS AND FOOD 23

    2.1.1 Lunar New Year Celebrations 23

    2.1.2 Mid-Autumn Festival Delicacies 24

2.2 TEA CULTURE AND TEA CUISINE 25

    2.2.1 Origins and Significance 25

    2.2.2 Tea Pairings and Rituals 26

2.3 DIM SUM AND STREET FOOD 27

    2.3.1 History of Dim Sum 28

    2.3.2 Street Food Culture in China 29

CHAPTER 3: ESSENTIAL EQUIPMENT FOR CHINESE COOKING 31

3.1 INTRODUCTION TO CHINESE KITCHEN TOOLS 31

    3.1.1 Woks and Stir-Fry Pans 31

    3.1.2 Cleavers and Knives 32

3.2 COOKING UTENSILS AND ACCESSORIES 33

    3.2.1 Bamboo Steamers and Racks 34

    3.2.2 Chinese Spider Skimmers 35

3.3 TIPS FOR SETTING UP YOUR CHINESE KITCHEN 36

    3.3.1 Organizing Ingredients and Utensils 36

    3.3.2 Creating a Functional Cooking Space 37

CHAPTER 4: CLASSIC CHINESE BREAKFASTS 39

4.1 CONGEE AND RICE PORRIDGE VARIETIES 39

4.1.1 Plain Congee (Zhou) 39

Eight-Treasure Congee (Babao Zhou)... 39

Ginger Infused Plain Congee (Zhou) 40

Chicken Ginger Congee 40

4.1.2 Century Egg Congee (Pidan Zhou) 40

Century Egg Tofu Congee 40

Ginger and Century Egg Porridge 40

Pork and Century Egg Congee 41

4.2 BREAKFAST DUMPLINGS AND BUNS 41

4.2.1 Shengjian Bao (Pan-Fried Soup Dumplings) 42

Shengjian Mantou (Pan-Fried Pork Buns) 42

Ji Dan Bing (Chinese Egg Pancake) 42

Luo Bo Si Bing (Radish Strips Pancake) 42

4.2.2 Char Siu Bao (Steamed BBQ Pork Buns) 43

Traditional Char Siu Bao (Steamed BBQ Pork Buns) 43

Golden Custard Buns (Liu Sha Bao) 43

Five Spice Chicken Buns (Wu Xiang Ji Bao) 43

4.3 CHINESE PANCAKES AND PASTRIES 44

4.3.1 Scallion Pancakes (Cong You Bing) 44

Five-Spice Tofu Pancakes 44

Classic Scallion Pancakes (Cong You Bing) 45

Red Bean Paste Pancakes 45

4.3.2 Red Bean Paste Pancakes (Hong Dou Bing) 45

Jasmine Tea Infused Red Bean Paste Pancakes 45

Savory Five-Spice Red Bean Pancakes 46

Coconut and Red Bean Paste Crêpes 46

CHAPTER 5: NOODLE DELIGHTS 47

5.1 HAND-PULLED AND KNIFE-CUT NOODLES 47

5.1.1 Lanzhou Beef Noodle Soup 47

Lanzhou Beef Noodle Soup 47

Xi'an Spicy Cumin Lamb Noodles 48

Guilin Rice Noodles with Braised Beef 48

5.1.2 Dao Xiao Mian (Knife-Cut Noodles) **48**

Traditional Shaanxi Biang Biang Noodles 48

Dao Xiao Mian with Pork and Bok Choy..49

Beef Shank Dao Xiao Mian 49

5.2 STIR-FRIED NOODLE DISHES **49**

5.2.1 Chow Mein with Vegetables **50**

Classic Vegetable Chow Mein 50

Spicy Szechuan Style Noodles..50

Stir-Fried Hoisin Noodles with Mixed Vegetables 51

5.2.2 Singapore Noodles **51**

Classic Singapore Noodles..51

Szechuan-Style Stir-Fry Noodles 51

Beijing Za Jiang Mian 52

5.3 NOODLE SOUPS AND BROTHS **52**

5.3.1 Wonton Noodle Soup **53**

Wonton Noodle Soup with Black Fungus and Bamboo Shoots 53

Ginger Scallion Wonton Soup 53

Spicy Sichuan Wonton Soup 54

5.3.2 Sichuan Spicy Hot Pot Noodles **54**

Sichuan Beef Hot Pot Noodles...54

Spicy Sichuan Chicken Noodle Soup..54

Mushroom and Tofu Hot Pot Noodles 55

CHAPTER 6: RICE CREATIONS **57**

6.1 STEAMED AND STICKY RICE DISHES **57**

6.1.1 Cantonese Sticky Rice (Lo Mai Gai) **57**

Cantonese Sticky Rice in Lotus Leaf (Lo Mai Gai) 57

Purple Yam and Sticky Rice Cake (Lo Mai Che) 58

Cantonese Sticky Rice (Lo Mai Gai) 58

6.1.2 Lotus Leaf Wrapped Rice (Luo Bo Gao) **58**

Jasmine Tea-Scented Lotus Leaf Rice 58

Lotus Leaf Wrapped Salted Egg Yolk Rice 59

Sweet Coconut and Red Bean Rice in Lotus Leaf 59

6.2 FRIED RICE VARIETIES **59**

6.2.1 Yangzhou Fried Rice **60**

Classic Yangzhou Fried Rice 60

Shandong Spiced Beef Fried Rice 60

Five Treasure Fried Rice 60

6.2.2 Pineapple Fried Rice **61**

Classic Pineapple Fried Rice 61

Thai Pineapple Fried Rice 61

Sichuan Pineapple Fried Rice 61

6.3 RICE PORRIDGE AND CONGEE RECIPES 62

6.3.1 Chicken and Corn Congee **62**

Ginger Chicken Congee 62

Mushroom and Chicken Congee 63

Century Egg and Lean Pork Congee 63

6.3.2 Preserved Egg and Pork Congee **63**

Ginger Chicken and Preserved Egg Congee 63

Beef and Ginger Congee 63

Mushroom and Preserved Egg Congee 64

CHAPTER 7: POULTRY PERFECTION 65

7.1 CHICKEN STIR-FRIES AND BRAISES 65

7.1.1 Kung Pao Chicken **65**

Kung Pao Chicken 65

Sichuan Pepper Chicken with Snow Peas 66

Honey-Glazed Chicken with Leeks 66

7.1.2 General Tso's Chicken **66**

Honey-Sesame General Tso's Chicken 66

Orange Zest General Tso's Chicken 67

Crispy Baked General Tso's Chicken 67

7.2 DUCK AND GOOSE DELICACIES 67

7.2.1 Peking Duck **68**

Traditional Peking Duck 68

Honey Glazed Peking Duck 68

Duck Breast with Plum Sauce 69

7.2.2 Cantonese Roast Duck **69**

Traditional Cantonese Roast Duck 69

Crispy Cantonese Duck 69

Five-Spice Duck Breast with Plum Sauce 70

7.3 FRAGRANT CHICKEN SOUPS AND BROTHS 70
7.3.1 Chinese Chicken and Sweet Corn Soup 70
Gingko Nut and Chicken Soup 70

Silkie Chicken Soup with Chinese Herbs 71

Chicken Soup with Lotus Seeds and Red Dates 71

7.3.2 Ginseng Chicken Soup 71
Ginseng Chicken Soup with Goji Berries 71

Black Chicken Ginseng Soup 72

Ginseng and Lotus Seed Chicken Soup 72

CHAPTER 8: PORK PLEASURES 73

8.1 SWEET AND SOUR PORK 73
8.1.1 Classic Sweet and Sour Pork 73
Honey Glazed Sweet and Sour Pork...73

Classic Sweet and Sour Pork 74

Szechuan Sweet and Sour Pork 74

8.1.2 Hong Shao Rou (Red-Braised Pork Belly) 74
Szechuan-Style Crispy Pork Belly..74

Honey Glazed Char Siu (Chinese BBQ Pork) 75

Black Bean Garlic Pork 75

8.2 PORK DUMPLINGS AND POTSTICKERS 75
8.2.1 Shui Jiao (Boiled Pork Dumplings) 76
Traditional Shui Jiao (Boiled Pork Dumplings) 76

Sichuan Style Shui Jiao 76

Ginger Pork Shui Jiao 77

8.2.2 Guo Tie (Pan-Fried Potstickers) 77
Traditional Pork Guo Tie (Pan-Fried Potstickers) 77

Sichuan Spicy Pork Guo Tie 77

Green Onion and Pork Guo Tie 78

8.3 SPICY PORK STIR-FRIES AND STEWS 78
8.3.1 Twice-Cooked Pork (Hui Guo Rou) 78
Szechuan Twice-Cooked Pork Belly..78

Fujian Style Twice-Cooked Pork 79

Hunan Smoked Pork with Leeks..79

8.3.2 Mapo Tofu with Minced Pork..79

Hunan Spicy Minced Pork 79

Sichuan Pork and Green Bean Stir-Fry...80

Ginger Pork Belly with Crispy Lotus Root..80

CHAPTER 9: BEEF BLISS...81

9.1 BEEF STIR-FRIES AND NOODLE DISHES...81

9.1.1 Mongolian Beef...81

Mongolian Beef with Black Bean Sauce 81

Szechuan Beef Stir-Fry...82

Beef and Broccoli with Garlic Sauce 82

9.1.2 Beef Chow Fun 82

Classic Beef Chow Fun 82

Spicy Sichuan Beef Chow Fun 83

Beef and Broccoli Chow Fun 83

9.2 BRAISED BEEF AND HOT POT..83

9.2.1 Chinese Braised Beef Shank 84

Anhui-Style Braised Beef Shank...84

Fujian Red Wine Braised Beef Shank..84

Hunan Spicy Braised Beef Shank..84

9.2.2 Sichuan Beef Hot Pot..85

Traditional Sichuan Beef Hot Pot...85

Sichuan Beef Tallow Hot Pot..85

Fiery Sichuan Broth Hot Pot 85

9.3 BEEF SOUPS AND BROTHS..86

9.3.1 Clear Beef Broth with Radish and Tofu 86

Clear Beef Broth with Radish and Tofu 86

Beef and Goji Berry Broth 87

Bok Choy and Beef Clear Soup..87

9.3.2 Spicy Beef Noodle Soup (Niurou Mian)...87

Sichuan Spicy Beef Noodle Soup..87

Beijing-Style Braised Beef Noodle Soup..87

Taiwanese Beef Noodle Soup..88

CHAPTER 10: SEAFOOD SENSATIONS 89

10.1 STIR-FRIED SEAFOOD SPECIALTIES 89

10.1.1 Salt and Pepper Shrimp 89

Salt and Pepper Shrimp with a Twist 89

Ginger Scallion Lobster 89

Szechuan Spicy Octopus 90

10.1.2 Garlic Butter Lobster 90

Sichuan-Style Garlic Butter Lobster 90

Cantonese Lobster with Garlic and Oyster Sauce 90

Szechuan Spicy Garlic Lobster 91

10.2 STEAMED FISH AND SEAFOOD DIM SUM 91

10.2.1 Cantonese Steamed Fish (Diu Zi Yu) 92

Cantonese Steamed Fish (Diu Zi Yu) 92

Soy-Ginger Steamed Scallops 92

Black Bean Sauce Steamed Cod 92

10.2.2 Shrimp Dumplings (Har Gow) 93

Classic Har Gow (Shrimp Dumplings) 93

Squid Ink Siu Mai 93

Jade Dumplings 93

10.3 SEAFOOD SOUPS AND CONGEE 94

10.3.1 Chinese Fish Soup with Tofu and Vegetables 94

Silver Carp Soup with Pickled Vegetables and Tofu 94

Braised Sea Bass with Shiitake Mushrooms and Bamboo Shoots 94

Tofu and Seaweed Soup with Clams 95

10.3.2 Seafood Congee with Scallops and Shrimp 95

Scallops and Shrimp Seafood Congee 95

Ginger Lobster Congee 95

Abalone Mushroom Seafood Congee 96

CHAPTER 11: SWEET ENDINGS 97

11.1 TRADITIONAL CHINESE DESSERTS 97

11.1.1 Red Bean Paste Buns (Dou Sha Bao) 97

Red Bean Paste Buns (Dou Sha Bao) 97

Black Sesame Seed Buns 97

Lotus Seed Paste Buns 98

11.1.2 Egg Custard Tarts (Dan Tat) **98**

Black Sesame Egg Custard Tarts 98

Ginger Honey Egg Custard Tarts 98

Jasmine Tea Egg Custard Tarts 99

11.2 FRUIT-BASED SWEETS AND TREATS **99**

11.2.1 Mango Pudding **99**

Lychee and Mango Pudding 99

Dragon Fruit and Pineapple Gelato 100

Chilled Kumquat and Honey Soup 100

11.2.2 Coconut Sticky Rice with Mango **100**

Mango and Coconut Jelly Squares 100

Tropical Mango Coconut Ice Cream 100

Mango Coconut Rice Pudding 101

11.3 MODERN TWISTS ON CLASSIC DESSERTS **101**

11.3.1 Green Tea Matcha Ice Cream **102**

Matcha Mochi Ice Cream 102

Sesame Matcha Ice Cream with Honey Swirl 102

Dragon Fruit and Matcha Ice Cream Bars 102

11.3.2 Black Sesame Seed Balls (Jian Dui) **102**

Matcha and Black Sesame Seed Balls 102

Chocolate-Coated Black Sesame Seed Balls 103

Cranberry and Black Sesame Brittle 103

CHAPTER 1: UNDERSTANDING CHINESE CUISINE

1.1 INTRODUCTION TO CHINESE CUISINE

Embarking on a culinary adventure into the heart of Chinese cuisine opens a treasure trove of flavors, techniques, and cultural significance. This introduction is your first step into a world where food is not just sustenance but an art form steeped in millennia of tradition. Chinese cuisine, with its diversity and depth, might initially seem daunting to the uninitiated. However, the secrets to mastering its delights are patience and a willingness to explore.

Imagine walking through the bustling markets of Chengdu, where the air is fragrant with the sizzle of Sichuan pepper and the sweet aroma of star anise. Each dish tells a story, not just of the region's abundant resources but also of its people and their history. The profound connection between Chinese society and its food is evident in every bite of tender Peking duck or each slurp of hearty, hand-pulled noodles.

For beginners, the complexities of Chinese cooking techniques can appear as intricate as the brush strokes of traditional Chinese calligraphy. Yet, just as with any art, beginning with the basics lays the foundation for future mastery. Understanding the balance of the five flavors—sweet, sour, salty, bitter, and umami—is essential. These are not just tastes but pathways to experiencing the Chinese way of life.

Moreover, the ingredients used in Chinese cuisine might seem unfamiliar but unlocking their potential is part of the joy. Each ingredient, from the humble soybean to the exotic lotus root, plays a crucial role in crafting dishes that are as nutritious as they are delicious. As you learn to embrace these elements, you'll discover not only the how but also the why behind each technique and recipe.

As we delve deeper into this chapter, remember that Chinese cuisine is a journey. Each meal is an opportunity to travel from the comfort of your kitchen to the ancient cities of China, where every dish is a celebration of life and heritage. So, gather your wok and chopsticks, and prepare to stir-fry, steam, and simmer your way through a culinary landscape that is as varied as it is rich. With each recipe, you will not just learn how to cook; you will learn how to weave the fabric of Chinese culture into your everyday meals.

1.1.1 HISTORY AND INFLUENCES

The intricate tapestry of Chinese cuisine, with its ancient flavors and profound traditions, is a story of civilization itself. Its history is woven through dynasties and regions, influenced by wars, trade, and the simple human delight in good food. To appreciate the depth of Chinese culinary traditions, we must journey back to its origins, exploring how each dynasty contributed its verse to the epic poem of Chinese cooking.

In the beginning, there was the millet and the rice, foundational grains first cultivated in the fertile Yellow River basin over 10,000 years ago. These grains became the cornerstone of Chinese society, just as bread did in the West. The ancient Chinese learned early on the importance of balancing their meals with a variety of flavors and nutrients, leading to the development of techniques like fermentation, which brought us soy sauce and vinegar—ingredients now synonymous with Chinese cooking.

As we meander through the Zhou Dynasty, we encounter the philosophical underpinnings that still influence Chinese cuisine today. It was during this era that the harmony of flavors, colors, and textures became central to the culinary arts, reflecting the Taoist quest for balance and Confucian ideals of order and respect. This period also saw the codification of the classic 'Five Flavors'—sweet, sour, salty, bitter, and umami—which chefs still consider essential for creating a balanced dish.

The Silk Road, that ancient network of trade routes, was as much a conveyor of spices as it was of silk and jade. Ingredients like cinnamon, cloves, and star anise made their way into the Chinese pantry, brought by caravans from the west. These spices were eagerly incorporated into existing recipes, adding new depths to already sophisticated flavor profiles.

During the Tang Dynasty, the imperial court's obsession with grand banquets led to further refinements in cooking techniques and presentation. The royal kitchen became a place of innovation, where chefs competed to please the emperor with elaborate dishes that were as beautiful to look at as they were delicious to eat. This era also welcomed the first major influences from abroad, particularly from Persia and Arabia, introducing new meat preparations and the idea of stuffing pastries, which would eventually evolve into dim sum.

The Song Dynasty brought an explosion of gastronomic literature, with scholars and cooks documenting recipes that detailed not just the ingredients but the philosophical and medicinal significance of each dish. It was also a time of economic prosperity and urban expansion, which saw the rise of restaurants and street food culture in cities like Kaifeng and Hangzhou. Here, the common people could taste dishes inspired by the imperial court, leading to a democratization of gourmet cuisine.

As we sail into the Ming and Qing dynasties, we see how the discovery of the New World impacted Chinese cuisine. The introduction of chili peppers, corn, and potatoes from the Americas revolutionized cooking styles, especially in regions like Sichuan and Hunan, where the hot and spicy flavors we associate with these areas today began to develop. Yet, the true essence of Chinese cooking lies not just in its techniques or ingredients but in its ability to tell the story of its people. From the humble farmer's simple rice porridge to the emperor's elaborate feasts, each dish is imbued with a sense of place and time, reflecting the land's abundance or the austerity of its seasons.

Through centuries of refinement and evolution, Chinese cuisine has maintained its core principles of balance, harmony, and seasonality. Today, as we explore these ancient recipes and techniques, we are not just cooking; we are reviving history, experiencing the same flavors that delighted emperors and nourished peasants alike. Each meal is a chapter from the past, inviting us to explore further and learn more.

In this exploration of Chinese cuisine's history and influences, we connect with a culture that has thrived through millenniums, adapting and evolving, but always retaining its identity. As modern cooks, we have the privilege to draw from this vast well of knowledge, using it to inform our practices and enrich our culinary experiences. By understanding where Chinese cooking has come from, we can appreciate its complexities and contribute to its ongoing story, ensuring that these ancient traditions continue to inspire and nourish generations to come.

1.1.2 REGIONAL VARIETIES

Travel through China's vast landscapes, and you'll discover that its culinary diversity mirrors its geographical and cultural variety. From the mist-covered mountains of Sichuan to the bustling streets of Shanghai, each region offers a distinct palate of flavors, ingredients, and cooking techniques that tell the story of its people and history. This journey through China's regional cuisines offers a glimpse into the rich tapestry of flavors that make Chinese cooking so uniquely complex and endlessly varied.

In the north, the food reflects the rugged climate, with wheat-based dishes like noodles, dumplings, and steamed buns dominating diets. The iconic Peking Duck from Beijing epitomizes the northern cooking philosophy—subtle seasoning designed to highlight the natural flavors of high-quality produce. The harsh winters led to the development of hearty, warming dishes and the use of preserving methods such as pickling and salting. Beijing, the imperial capital, cultivated a cuisine that is as refined as it is bold, with dishes like Zhajiangmian—a savory noodle dish topped with a thick sauce of fermented soybean paste and minced pork.

Travel east to Shandong, and you encounter a cuisine built around the bountiful seafood from the Yellow Sea. Here, the culinary style, known as Lu cuisine, is noted for its emphasis on freshness and tenderness. Soups and broths, clear and light yet flavorful, reflect the region's philosophy that the true taste of the sea needs no heavy masking. Dishes such as sweet and sour carp capture the essence of Shandong's culinary finesse.

As we venture to the eastern coastlines, Shanghai offers a sweeter twist to the typically saltier and oilier Eastern Chinese cuisine. Known for its delicate flavors and innovative use of ingredients, Shanghainese cuisine delights in the slow braising and red cooking techniques, where dishes like red-braised pork belly gently simmer in a mixture of soy sauce, sugar, and rice wine, creating a harmoniously rich flavor.

Journeying south, we enter the culinary heartland of Cantonese cooking, prevalent in the Guangdong region and Hong Kong. This cuisine is characterized by its wide range and balance of flavors and a profound emphasis on preserving the natural taste of the ingredients. Dim sum, literally meaning 'touch the heart,' is perhaps the most famous Cantonese culinary export. These small bite-sized portions, served in bamboo steamers, range from delicate shrimp dumplings to rich, savory char siu bao (barbecue pork buns). The subtlety of steaming—a favorite cooking method in the south—exemplifies the Cantonese commitment to freshness.

Further inland, the mountains and misty landscapes of Sichuan are home to one of China's most bold and fiery cuisines. Sichuanese cooking is famous for its liberal use of garlic, chili peppers, and the unique Sichuan peppercorn, which together produce a tingling sensation known as málà. Dishes like mapo tofu and kung pao chicken are not just meals; they are experiences, intense and explosive, reflecting the spirited nature of Sichuan's people and culture.

Moving to the central plains, Hunan cuisine offers a similar heat to Sichuan but with a sour tang, a testament to the local love for pickled foods and vinegar. Hunan's chefs prefer smoking and curing, techniques well-suited to a region that experiences both sweltering summers and chilly winters. The result is a robust cuisine that is hearty and heavily seasoned, exemplified in dishes like Dong'an chicken.

Each region of China contributes its verse to the grand culinary epic of the nation. These regional varieties are not just about taste and technique; they are a dialogue with the environment and history, an expression of cultural identity through food. As such, understanding Chinese cuisine in its regional contexts allows us not only to appreciate the diversity and sophistication of Chinese cooking but also to glimpse the interplay of geography, climate, history, and culture that shapes the daily lives of its people.

The journey through China's regional cuisines is as much an exploration of flavor as it is a voyage across time and culture. Each dish tells a story, and each story is a reminder of how deeply food is intertwined with the human experience. As we explore these regions and their recipes, we are invited not just to cook but to taste the history and geography of one of the world's greatest civilizations. This exploration is not simply about learning to prepare dishes; it is about understanding a rich cultural heritage and how it can be expressed through the simple act of cooking and sharing food.

1.2 EXPLORING CANTONESE CUISINE

As we delve into the refined and subtle world of Cantonese cuisine, we uncover a culinary tradition that embodies sophistication and a profound reverence for ingredients. Originating from Guangdong province in southern China, this cuisine is a testament to the region's bountiful coasts and fertile lands, which offer an abundant array of fresh produce and seafood. Renowned for its elegant and understated approach, Cantonese cooking is less about the bold interplay of flavors seen in other Chinese regional cuisines and more about enhancing the natural essence of its components.

In this exploration, we will discover how Cantonese chefs have mastered the art of steaming and stir-frying, techniques that accentuate the ingredient's own flavors without overwhelming them. We'll also take a closer look at the tradition of Yum Cha, a delightful culinary practice that combines the pleasures of taste and social enjoyment through dim sum. This part of the journey not only introduces us to iconic dishes like har gow (shrimp dumplings) and siu mai (pork dumplings) but also invites us to partake in the ceremonial tea service that accompanies these meals, reflecting the region's ethos of living harmoniously.

Join me as we taste our way through Cantonese cuisine, where each dish serves as a delicate poem, quietly but confidently expressing the rich narrative of its homeland.

1.2.1 CHARACTERISTICS AND FLAVORS

Cantonese cuisine, originating from the Guangdong region in southern China, is celebrated for its exceptional finesse and the purity of its flavors. Known as one of the Eight Culinary Traditions of Chinese cuisine, it stands out for its lightness and balance, emphasizing fresh ingredients and subtle seasonings that enhance rather than mask the natural taste of the food. This cuisine reflects the Cantonese philosophy of "qing dan" which means light and fresh, a principle that guides every dish, from the selection of ingredients to the final garnish.

In Cantonese cooking, the freshness of ingredients is paramount. The proximity of the region to the South China Sea provides a steady supply of seafood, making it a staple in the local diet. The Cantonese are experts in extracting the sweet essence of seafood, evident in dishes such as steamed fish, seasoned simply with soy sauce, scallions, and a sprinkle of fresh ginger. The method of steaming, favored in Cantonese kitchens, preserves the ingredient's original flavors and textures, presenting them in their most natural and pure form.

Another hallmark of Cantonese cuisine is its variety of cooking techniques, which include steaming, stir-frying, shallow frying, double boiling, and braising. Each technique is chosen with care to suit the ingredient, ensuring that the natural flavors are not only preserved but also enhanced. For example, the stir-frying technique is fast and furious; it retains the crispness of vegetables while imbuing them with flavors from a hot wok, a dash of oil, and a splash of sauce.

Cantonese sauces and seasonings are used sparingly and with precision. Unlike the bold, spicy flavors of Sichuan cuisine, Cantonese dishes are more likely to seduce with a whisper than a shout. Classic seasonings include oyster sauce, hoisin sauce, black bean sauce, and a small amount of garlic and ginger. These are used not to overwhelm but to uplift the main ingredients. The art lies in the balance, achieving a harmonious dish where no single flavor dominates.

Dim sum, perhaps the most internationally recognized aspect of Cantonese cuisine, showcases this culinary artistry in miniature form. Originating from the Cantonese tradition of 'Yum Cha' or drinking tea, dim sum includes a variety of small, delicate bites ranging from dumplings to buns and pastries. Each piece is crafted to offer a balance of flavor, texture, and aroma. The experience of dim sum is also a social one, with families and friends gathering to share these treats over leisurely conversations and tea. This communal aspect highlights the Cantonese appreciation for food not only as nourishment but as a means to foster community and connection.

The sweetness in Cantonese dishes often comes from natural ingredients rather than added sugars. Fruits such as lychees, longans, and certain kinds of melons are incorporated into meals either in savory dishes or as desserts. Even in meat dishes, such as char siu (barbecued pork), the sweetness is typically derived from honey used in the marinade, which caramelizes during cooking to create a beautifully rich and glossy exterior that is as pleasing to the eye as it is to the palate.

Soups hold a special place in Cantonese cuisine, often served as a starter to meals. These are not the thick, hearty soups seen in other cultures but are instead clear and light, yet rich in flavor. They are made by simmering meat and vegetables over low heat for several hours, allowing all the flavors to meld into a delicate broth. Ingredients like goji berries, lotus seeds, and jujubes are frequently added for their health benefits, reflecting the Cantonese commitment to food that is as beneficial to the body as it is delightful to the taste buds.

In the world of Cantonese desserts, the approach is equally restrained. Sweets are often less sugary than their Western counterparts, with a subtle sweetness that comes from ingredients like red beans, sesame seeds, or sweet potatoes. Desserts such as mango pudding or sweet tofu pudding (douhua) are popular endings to a meal, providing a refreshing and light finish that cleanses the palate rather than overwhelming it with sugar.

Through these characteristics and flavors, Cantonese cuisine invites diners into a world where every ingredient matters, and every dish tells a story of refinement and care. It is a cuisine that does not rely on complexity but rather seeks to elevate simplicity to an art form, where the true essence of each component is allowed to shine. This approach not only makes Cantonese food a delight to eat but also a profound expression of the culture from which it comes. As we explore these dishes, we do more than just taste them; we learn about the people, the landscape, and the history that have shaped this exquisite culinary tradition.

1.2.2 POPULAR CANTONESE DISHES

In the world of Cantonese cuisine, the dishes are not merely meals; they are stories of cultural heritage, craftsmanship, and the delicate balance of flavor that define southern China's culinary landscape. Each dish, from the humble congee to the complex flavors of char siu, carries with it a history as rich and layered as the region itself.

Char Siu (Barbecued Pork) is arguably one of the most iconic representations of Cantonese cooking. This dish features pork shoulder or loin that has been marinated in a mixture of honey, five-spice powder, red fermented bean curd, dark soy sauce, and a touch of hoisin. The pork is then barbecued or roasted to caramelized perfection. The result is slices of pork that are irresistibly sweet on the outside and tenderly savory on the inside, often served with a simple side of steamed rice or noodles to complement its robust flavors.

Dim Sum, meaning 'touch the heart,' consists of a variety of small, bite-sized portions served in bamboo steamers or on small plates. This culinary practice is as much about the social experience as it is about eating. Traditional dim sum includes dishes like **Har Gow** (delicate shrimp dumplings with a translucent wrapper), **Siu Mai** (open-topped dumplings filled with shrimp and pork), and **Char Siu Bao** (fluffy buns filled with barbecued pork). Each piece is crafted to offer not just a taste but a tactile experience, from the smooth, soft exterior of a dumpling to the rich, dense filling inside.

Congee is a type of rice porridge that epitomizes comfort food in Cantonese cuisine. Often eaten as a breakfast or a light meal, congee is cooked until the rice is completely broken down and has a silky, creamy consistency. It can be served plain or embellished with a variety of toppings like minced beef, century eggs, or finely chopped green onions. Congee is not only a testament to the Cantonese ability to transform simple ingredients into nourishing meals but also represents a meal that is both healing and fortifying.

Steamed Fish, particularly the steamed whole fish, is a testament to the Cantonese mastery of seafood. The fish, often a white-fleshed variety like snapper, is steamed with nothing more than ginger, scallions, and a splash of soy sauce. The technique highlights the fish's delicate flesh and sweet marine flavors, enhanced subtly by the aromatics. In Cantonese culture, serving a whole fish is also a symbol of prosperity and completeness, often featured in celebratory meals and special occasions.

Roast Goose is another celebratory dish, known for its crispy skin and succulent meat. The goose is marinated in a blend of spices and ingredients like star anise, ginger, spring onion, and soy sauce, then roasted to achieve a perfectly crispy skin while keeping the inside juicy and flavorful. It's typically served with plum sauce or a simple mixture of salt and pepper to enhance its natural flavors.

Sweet and Sour Pork, though found in many regional Chinese cuisines, has a distinctive Cantonese version known as "Gu Lao Rou." This dish features pork that is first deep-fried to a golden crisp and then stir-fried with a sweet and sour sauce made from sugar, ketchup, vinegar, and soy sauce. The sauce's bright, tangy flavor complements the crispy pork, often accompanied by bell peppers and pineapple for an added layer of complexity.

In Cantonese desserts, **Mango Pudding** stands out for its refreshing sweetness. Made from ripe mangoes, gelatin, and cream, this pudding is smooth and luscious, capturing the essence of tropical flavor that pairs beautifully with the heavier savory dishes.

These dishes, popular not only in Guangdong and Hong Kong but around the world, illustrate the global appeal of Cantonese cuisine. They convey the principles of balance, subtlety, and freshness that are hallmarks of the region's cooking. Each dish offers a glimpse into the culinary philosophy of Canton, where food is an art that nurtures the body, delights the senses, and honors the richness of its cultural heritage.

Exploring these popular Cantonese dishes is more than a culinary exercise; it's an immersion into a culture that values precision, respect for ingredients, and a deep-rooted sense of community. Through these flavors, we learn not just about a region's dietary preferences but about its history, its celebrations, and its everyday life. As we taste our way through these dishes, we partake in a centuries-old tradition that continues to evolve and inspire, bridging the past with the present in every bite.

1.3 CONTRASTING CHINESE AND CANTONESE COOKING

In the rich tapestry of Chinese cuisine, Cantonese cooking shines as a beacon of subtlety and refinement amidst the vast and diverse culinary practices of China. As we explore the contrasts between Cantonese and broader Chinese culinary approaches, we uncover not only the distinctions in flavor, technique, and ingredients but also the cultural nuances that define regional identities within this sprawling nation.

Cantonese cuisine, known for its delicate balance and light seasoning, emphasizes the inherent flavors of the freshest ingredients, whether from the land or the sea. This approach stands in contrast to the bold, often spicy flavors of Sichuan or the hearty, wheat-based dishes of northern China. Here, the art of steaming and stir-frying is perfected to enhance natural tastes without overpowering them, a philosophy that speaks to the Cantonese reverence for purity and tradition.

This sub-chapter delves into these culinary contrasts, exploring how historical migrations, geographical differences, and cultural exchanges have shaped the cooking methods and flavor profiles unique to each Chinese region. Through this comparative lens, we appreciate the individuality of Cantonese cuisine as a part of the greater Chinese culinary landscape, offering a deeper understanding of how regional characteristics influence and enrich the collective gastronomic heritage of China.

1.3.1 INGREDIENTS AND FLAVOR PROFILES

As we delve into the intricate world of Chinese cuisine, it becomes apparent that the landscape of ingredients and flavor profiles is as varied as the country's geography. Each region, with its unique climate and cultural influences, has developed a distinct culinary identity. Cantonese cuisine, in particular, showcases a stark contrast to the broader Chinese cooking practices through its meticulous selection of ingredients and subtle flavor enhancements.

Cantonese cooking, originating from the humid, subtropical region of Guangdong, has access to an abundant variety of fresh produce, seafood, and livestock. This bounty is reflected in the minimalistic approach to seasoning, which aims to highlight the natural flavors of the ingredients rather than mask them. Freshness is the cornerstone of Cantonese cuisine, with markets bustling daily with live fish, shellfish, and a vibrant assortment of greens. In contrast, regions such as Sichuan or Hunan rely heavily on the preservative qualities of spices and oils, stemming from historical necessities where fresh ingredients were not always available year-round.

One of the quintessential elements of Cantonese flavor is the subtle use of sauces and seasonings. Light soy sauce, oyster sauce, and a hint of sesame oil often suffice to enhance flavors without overwhelming the senses. This differs significantly from the robust, often fiery profiles found in Northern and Western Chinese cuisines, where ingredients like star anise, Sichuan peppercorn, and black vinegar dominate. These stronger flavors cater to colder climates, providing warmth and stimulation to the palate.

Moreover, the Cantonese penchant for soups and broths exemplifies the region's culinary ethos. A well-prepared Cantonese soup is clear and light, yet rich in flavor, often simmered for hours with chicken, pork bones, or seafood alongside herbs and vegetables. This method extracts deep flavors in a subtle broth, believed not only to nourish the body but also to offer medicinal benefits. In contrast, soups in Northern China are often heartier, thicker, and include ingredients like noodles or dumplings, serving as a meal's centerpiece rather than a delicate prelude.

The art of steaming in Cantonese cuisine also highlights the region's culinary finesse. Steamed fish, a staple in Cantonese households, is typically dressed with nothing more than shredded ginger, scallions, and a splash of soy sauce before being cooked to perfection. This technique preserves the fish's delicate texture and the sweet taste of the sea, unlike the braised or stewed fish preparations common in Eastern Chinese provinces, which often feature heavier, more aromatic sauces.

Dim sum, another jewel in the Cantonese culinary crown, offers a glimpse into the precision and variety of the region's cooking. Small bites like shrimp dumplings (har gow) and pork siu mai are prepared so that each ingredient, no matter how minute, can be tasted distinctly. This contrasts sharply with the more robust, often spicier flavors of street foods from regions like Shanghai or Chengdu, where boldness and depth of flavor are prioritized.

In sweets and desserts, Cantonese cuisine tends to favor subtlety and lightness as well. Desserts such as almond jelly and mango pudding are gently sweetened, often deriving hints of flavor from fruits or nuts rather than heavy syrups or creams. This approach starkly contrasts with the richer, more robust sweets of Northern China, like sesame balls or sweetened bean pastes, which cater to a palate seeking denser, heartier textures and flavors.

This exploration of ingredients and flavor profiles not only delineates the culinary distinctions between Cantonese and other Chinese cuisines but also paints a broader picture of China's regional diversity. Through this palette of tastes and techniques, we see a narrative of people and place, of climate and culture, each influencing and defining the ways food is prepared and enjoyed. As we savor these flavors, we learn more than just recipes; we uncover stories of survival, adaptation, and ultimate refinement, illustrating the profound connection between a people and their food.

1.3.2 COOKING TECHNIQUES AND TRADITIONS

Within the intricate web of Chinese culinary practices, the difference in cooking techniques and traditions between regions is profound, with Cantonese cuisine embodying a style that is both a testament to the region's historical prosperity and a reflection of its climatic advantages. This sub-chapter delves into these unique aspects of Cantonese cooking, contrasting them with the broader array of methods found throughout China, each shaped by distinct historical, environmental, and cultural factors.

Cantonese cooking techniques are characterized by their refinement and precision, focusing on enhancing the natural flavors of the ingredients without masking them. Steaming, an essential technique in Cantonese kitchens, perfectly illustrates this approach. Unlike the heavy frying and robust spicing typical of Northern and Western Chinese cuisines, steaming allows the delicate flavors of the freshest fish, poultry, and vegetables to shine through. This method not only preserves the ingredients' nutritional value but also highlights their inherent qualities, a priority in the Cantonese culinary philosophy.

Stir-frying, another cornerstone of Cantonese technique, is performed over high heat for a very short time. This method is about precision and speed—vegetables and meats are cut finely to ensure they cook quickly and evenly, retaining their texture and color. The stir-fry technique contrasts sharply with the slow braising and stewing practices seen in other Chinese regions, where flavors are built over hours and the ingredients often meld into a single harmonious blend.

Roasting and barbecuing are also prominent in Cantonese cuisine, with dishes such as roast goose and char siu being prime examples. These techniques, which require control over heat and timing, reflect the Cantonese penchant for crisp, caramelized exteriors and tender, flavorful interiors. Such dishes are celebrated not just for their taste but for their appearance and aroma, engaging all the senses.

Dim sum preparation showcases yet another facet of Cantonese culinary artistry. The making of dim sum involves a variety of techniques from steaming to frying, each chosen to complement the filling and wrapping of choice. This contrasts with the more straightforward preparation methods of dumplings in Northern China, where the focus is often on the dough's texture and the robust flavors of the fillings, rather than on a complex array of cooking styles.

Broth-making in Cantonese cuisine is an all-day affair that contrasts with the quicker soup preparations seen elsewhere. The broths are clear and light yet imbued with deep, extracted flavors from their ingredients, achieved through hours of simmering at a controlled temperature. This method stands in stark contrast to the often thicker, heartier soups prepared in the colder northern regions, where soups are designed to provide warmth and energy.

The preservation techniques in Cantonese cooking, such as curing and drying, are less about necessity—given the region's mild climate and abundant resources—and more about enhancing flavors and textures in ingredients like sausages, preserved vegetables, and dried seafood. This is markedly different from the techniques used in harsher climates, where preservation is crucial for survival through severe winters.

In dessert preparation, Cantonese techniques continue to emphasize subtlety and lightness, with sweets often steamed or lightly fried and not overly sweetened. This is a departure from the richer, heavier desserts found in other parts of China, where deep-frying and thick, sweet sauces dominate.

Through these diverse cooking methods, Cantonese cuisine not only distinguishes itself from other Chinese culinary traditions but also tells a story of its environment, culture, and history. It speaks to a society that has had the luxury of focusing on culinary finesse due to its rich natural resources and favorable climate, contrasting with regions where food preparation techniques evolved out of necessity and environmental challenges.

These techniques are not just methods of preparing food but are also expressions of cultural identity and regional pride. They offer a lens through which the social fabric of the Cantonese people can be viewed, reflecting values of family, community, and the celebration of life's finer details. As such, exploring Cantonese cooking techniques and traditions provides not only culinary insight but also a deeper understanding of the human experience behind the cuisine.

CHAPTER 2: CHINESE CULINARY TRADITIONS

2.1 FESTIVALS AND FOOD

In the vibrant tapestry of Chinese culture, food not only sustains the body but also enriches every festival and celebration, weaving together flavors and traditions that date back thousands of years. Chinese festivals are exuberant, colorful expressions of cultural heritage, where each dish served is imbued with symbolism and history, designed to bring luck, prosperity, and joy to all who partake in the feast.

As we explore the relationship between festivals and food in Chinese culinary traditions, we enter a world where each bite tells a story of seasonal cycles, historical events, and communal values. The Lunar New Year, for instance, is unthinkable without the reunion dinner, a lavish meal meant to fortify family ties and ensure a auspicious start to the year. Mooncakes during the Mid-Autumn Festival not only represent the full moon but also the fullness of life, sharing, and unity.

This sub-chapter will delve into how these traditional foods are prepared, enjoyed, and the meanings they carry, offering insights into not just the how, but the why behind these culinary practices. Through this journey, we'll see how deeply food is interwoven with joy and tradition in Chinese society, and how festivals serve as a conduit for passing these culinary legacies from one generation to the next.

2.1.1 LUNAR NEW YEAR CELEBRATIONS

The Lunar New Year, or Spring Festival, is perhaps the most exuberant and deeply cherished of all the Chinese festivals. It marks not just the turn of the traditional lunisolar Chinese calendar but also symbolizes new beginnings and the renewal of family bonds. Central to these celebrations is the food, which is steeped in symbolism and crafted with meticulous care to ensure prosperity and happiness for the coming year.

At the heart of Lunar New Year festivities is the reunion dinner, held on the eve of the New Year. This meal is arguably the most important dinner of the year, bringing together family members from far and wide. The dishes served are chosen for their symbolic meanings, derived from their names or appearances which connote wishes for the family's future.

One of the quintessential dishes is the fish, served whole, and often steamed. In Chinese, the word for fish, "yu," sounds like the word for surplus. Serving a whole fish represents a wish for abundance, and leaving some of the fish uneaten forecasts accumulated wealth. Another indispensable dish is the dumpling, shaped like ancient Chinese gold or silver ingots. Traditionally made and consumed during the reunion dinner, dumplings symbolize wealth; the more dumplings one eats at the New Year celebration, the more money they can hope to make in the upcoming year.

Noodles also play a critical role in New Year celebrations. Long, uncut noodles represent longevity and life; hence, they are served to wish family members a long and healthy life. The preparation is simple, often stir-fried with vegetables, to maintain focus on their length and continuity.

Another popular dish is "nian gao," or rice cake, which is believed to bring good luck. The name "nian gao" sounds like it means "higher year," and it is eaten with the hope of achieving greater heights in the days to come, whether in terms of one's career, school performance, or the physical growth of one's children.

Not to be forgotten are the sweet treats that are omnipresent during the New Year. Candied fruits, sesame balls, and "fa gao" (a fluffy steamed cake that signifies prosperity because the word "fa" means both "prosperity" and "to raise") are popular choices. These desserts are not only enjoyed for their flavors but are also offered to ancestors and gods in various rituals during the festival.

Additionally, the Lunar New Year is marked by various customs that involve food. For example, on the first day of the New Year, it is customary to avoid meat, a practice believed to ensure long and happy lives. This day is often reserved for vegetarian dishes, which is a nod to Buddhist traditions that suggest clean living and respect for all living beings.

The Lunar New Year's connection to food extends beyond the home. Food also plays a part in welcoming the gods of wealth and prosperity. On the fifth day, when it is believed that the God of Wealth visits households, dumplings are eaten in northern China, while sweet rice balls are consumed in the south, each region with its variation in hopes of currying favor and ensuring a prosperous year.

These culinary traditions, rich with meaning and festivity, are not just a feast for the senses but a vital part of reinvigorating family ties and communal spirit. They reaffirm social bonds and cultural identity, weaving a collective narrative of hope and renewal. Through these foods, each family passes on its wishes for the future, making the Lunar New Year a profound communal and culinary experience, celebrated with both reverence and joy across Chinese communities worldwide.

2.1.2 MID-AUTUMN FESTIVAL DELICACIES

The Mid-Autumn Festival, known as Zhongqiu Jie in China, is a poignant celebration of harvest and familial bonds, marked by the appreciation of the moon at its fullest and brightest. This festival, which falls on the 15th day of the eighth lunar month, is a time when families reunite to give thanks for the harvest and pray for good fortune. Central to these celebrations are the foods, rich in symbolism and tradition, which are prepared and enjoyed together.

Perhaps the most iconic of all Mid-Autumn Festival foods is the mooncake. This delicacy is not merely a treat; it's a deep-rooted cultural symbol of unity and completeness. Mooncakes are round, symbolizing the full moon and completeness of the gathering family. Their meticulous preparation and detailed designs reflect the care and value placed on this festive gathering. Traditionally filled with lotus seed paste and salted egg yolks, which represent the moon, these cakes are shared among family and friends to signify the sharing of luck and happiness.

Beyond mooncakes, the festival table features a variety of foods that are selected for their symbolic meanings. Pomelos are eaten and placed on altars, as their Chinese name, 'youzi', sounds similar to 'blessing'. Eating pomelos is believed to bring continuous prosperity and status, as well as family unity, because the Chinese word for pomelo suggests the togetherness of family members.

Crabs are another seasonal delicacy during the Mid-Autumn Festival, particularly the hairy crab, which is at its fattest and most flavorful at this time of year. The crab's round shape and patterning of its shell also echo the full moon, making it a fitting addition to the celebration. It is enjoyed not just for its delicious taste but for its health benefits, as it is believed to enhance yin, or cooling energy, in the body.

Taro is another food traditionally consumed during this festival, often steamed or made into sweet dishes. It is believed to bring good luck and prosperity to the family. The starchy root is a staple in many Asian cuisines and its inclusion in the Mid-Autumn Festival is a nod to agricultural roots and the importance of the harvest.

Another significant aspect of the Mid-Autumn Festival is the consumption of tea, particularly oolong or green tea, which complements the rich flavors of the mooncakes and aids in digestion. The act of sharing tea reflects a gesture of peace and reflects the tranquility of the moonlit evening.

These foods are more than just components of a meal; they are imbued with layers of meaning and tradition. Each dish is chosen not only for its seasonal appropriateness but also for its deeper significance to the festival's themes of reunion, thanksgiving, and the celebration of the cyclical nature of life.

Furthermore, the festival is also an occasion for lanterns, which are carried by children or hung in temples and homes. These lanterns are often elaborately decorated with symbols from folklore and serve as an additional luminary complement to the moon, creating a magical atmosphere that enhances the evening's celebrations.

The Mid-Autumn Festival's culinary traditions provide a vivid insight into Chinese cultural values, where food is an expression of more than sustenance but a medium of heritage and familial bonds. As families gather under the moonlight, sharing these special foods, they reinforce the cultural fabric that has been woven through generations. This festival is a celebration of the abundance of the harvest, the beauty of the cosmos, and the warmth of family— all shared through the foods that grace the tables of celebrating families across the country and beyond.

2.2 TEA CULTURE AND TEA CUISINE

In the realm of Chinese culture, tea is more than a mere beverage; it is a profound cultural artifact, intertwined with history, philosophy, and the culinary arts. The tradition of tea in China stretches back millennia, evolving from a medicinal concoction to an essential component of daily life and social ceremony. As we delve into the world of tea culture and tea cuisine, we explore not only the varieties and brewing techniques of tea but also its significant role in Chinese dining and social rituals.

Tea culture in China is characterized by its diversity, with each region boasting its own unique traditions and tea varieties—from the robust flavors of Pu-erh in Yunnan to the delicate fragrances of Green tea in Zhejiang. This sub-chapter will not only introduce these varieties but also explore how tea is seamlessly integrated into meals, enhancing flavors and aiding digestion, creating what is known as tea cuisine.

This intricate dance of tea and food is a testament to the Chinese pursuit of harmony and balance, both in flavor and in life. Join us as we steep ourselves in the aromatic world of Chinese tea, where each sip resonates with centuries of tradition and each dish tells a story of culinary refinement.

2.2.1 ORIGINS AND SIGNIFICANCE

Tea, the quintessential Chinese elixir, has permeated the fabric of China's history and culture in profound ways. Its story begins in the mist-shrouded mountains of ancient China, where it was first discovered and later transformed from a medicinal herb to a symbol of cultural sophistication and a daily necessity. Understanding the origins and significance of tea in Chinese culture provides a deeper appreciation of not just the beverage itself but also its pivotal role in social customs, health, and culinary practices.

Legend has it that tea was discovered by Emperor Shen Nong in 2737 BC, a mythical ruler and skilled scientist who decreed that all drinking water be boiled as a health precaution. One day, as he rested under a wild tea tree with boiling water at his side, a few leaves drifted into the pot. Intrigued by the delightful aroma, Shen Nong tasted the infusion and found it refreshing, thus heralding the birth of tea.

From these mythic origins, tea's journey through Chinese history is marked by its evolution into a beverage enjoyed by all strata of society. During the Tang Dynasty, tea became a popular drink among the nobility and the subject of the first known monograph on tea, "The Classic of Tea," written by the scholar Lu Yu. This period solidified tea's status in Chinese culture, embedding it deeply within daily life and leading to the creation of the tea ceremony, which emphasized precision, reverence, and the aesthetic pleasure of tea drinking.

By the time of the Song Dynasty, tea culture had evolved further, with the invention of powdered tea and the development of elaborate tea ceremonies, which were akin to performance art. Tea drinking had become a refined, artistic pursuit that mirrored the sophistication of the era. Tea houses began to spring up, becoming centers of social interaction and cultural expression.

The Ming Dynasty heralded significant changes in the way tea was consumed, with the transition from powdered to loose-leaf tea. This shift led to the development of new brewing techniques and the popularization of the gaiwan—a lidded bowl used for infusing and drinking tea. During this era, tea cultivation spread throughout China, leading to the discovery and development of various tea varieties, each with its unique flavor profile, which were treasured across the land and beyond.

The significance of tea in Chinese culture extends beyond its role as a beverage. It is a medium for social bonding and an expression of hospitality. Serving tea is a sign of respect, a gesture of welcome to guests that transcends social classes. Moreover, the Chinese tea ceremony, with its meticulous preparation and serene execution, reflects the Daoist principles of harmony between humans and nature, encouraging mindfulness, and appreciation of the moment.

In the realm of health, tea has been revered for its medicinal properties since ancient times. Traditional Chinese medicine prescribes tea for its cooling properties to counteract excess heat in the body, improve digestion, and detoxify the system. Different types of tea are believed to offer various health benefits, influencing everything from energy levels to mental clarity.

Culinarily, tea has also found its place in the Chinese kitchen, not just as a beverage but as a cooking ingredient. Tea-smoked duck and green tea-infused desserts are just a couple of examples of how tea's robust and delicate flavors are harnessed in Chinese cuisine. The practice of using tea leaves in cooking demonstrates the versatility of this ingredient and reflects the Chinese knack for integrating various elements of their culture.

Today, tea remains a vital part of Chinese life, celebrated during traditional festivals, used in ceremonies to honor ancestors, and enjoyed in the daily rhythm of life, from bustling city tea houses to quiet rural gardens. Its enduring presence is a testament to its ingrained importance in Chinese culture—a bridge from the past to the present, carrying centuries of history in each leaf and sip.

Exploring the origins and significance of tea illuminates more than the storied past of a beverage; it reveals the soul of Chinese culture, showcasing how a simple leaf brewed in water has shaped social customs, health beliefs, and culinary traditions across millennia.

2.2.2 TEA PAIRINGS AND RITUALS

In the rich tapestry of Chinese tea culture, the art of pairing tea with food and the intricate rituals that accompany its preparation and consumption are as important as the tea itself. These practices not only enhance the gastronomic experience but also embody the philosophical depth of Chinese culture, emphasizing balance, harmony, and mindfulness.

Tea Pairings: An Art Form

The pairing of tea with food is an art that seeks to complement and contrast flavors, creating a harmonious dining experience. Just as wine pairing is celebrated in Western gastronomy, tea pairing holds a place of honor in Chinese cuisine. The right tea can elevate a meal, cleanse the palate, aid in digestion, and enhance the flavors of the accompanying dishes.

- **Green Tea**: Known for its delicate and slightly astringent flavor, green tea pairs beautifully with light dishes such as steamed fish, salads, or chicken. The subtle grassy notes of green tea can refresh the palate and enhance the meal's inherent flavors without overwhelming them.
- **Oolong Tea**: The complex flavor profile of Oolong, which can range from fruity to woody, makes it versatile for pairing with a variety of foods. It is particularly effective with spicy dishes or fatty meats like roasted duck. The tea's robust body and aromatic fragrance can counterbalance the richness and spice, creating a balanced taste experience.

- **Black Tea**: With its bold and sometimes malty flavors, black tea is a good match for heavier, more flavorful dishes such as red meat or oily fried foods. It can stand up to strong flavors and helps cut through the fat, cleansing the palate.
- **Pu-erh Tea**: Aged Pu-erh is appreciated for its deep, earthy quality and is traditionally paired with highly flavorful dishes, including barbecued meats and flavorful mushrooms. Its unique fermentation process and rich taste profile make it ideal for offsetting the heaviness of these dishes.

Rituals of Tea: Cultivating Mindfulness and Community

The rituals surrounding tea preparation and consumption are as varied as the regions of China itself, each reflecting local customs and the philosophical leanings of the culture. Central to all these rituals, however, is the principle of mindfulness—focusing on the present moment and appreciating the simplicity and subtlety of the tea.

- **Gongfu Tea Ceremony**: This elaborate tea brewing process is a meditation in mindfulness and an exhibition of skill. Practiced primarily in the Fujian and Guangdong provinces, the Gongfu ceremony uses small teapots and cups to emphasize the aesthetic pleasure of tea drinking. The ritual involves multiple infusions of the same leaves, each designed to draw out a different aspect of the tea's flavor profile. This ceremony is not just about drinking tea; it's about celebrating the tea's taste, aroma, and the company of fellow participants.
- **Tea and Incense Pairing**: In some parts of China, tea rituals incorporate the burning of incense, creating an atmosphere that engages all the senses. The aroma of the incense is chosen to complement the fragrance of the tea, enhancing the overall sensory experience and bringing a deeper level of relaxation and enjoyment.
- **Tea in Silence**: Among Buddhist practitioners, tea is often consumed in silence, allowing the drinker to fully immerse themselves in the experience, from the preparation to the last sip. This practice emphasizes the Zen principle of mindfulness, encouraging a deep connection with the present moment and a fuller appreciation of the tea.
- **Seasonal Tea Rituals**: The changing of seasons is often marked by special teas and ceremonies that reflect the time of year. Spring might be greeted with a fresh green tea, celebrating renewal, while autumn could be observed with a rich black tea, symbolizing the coming cold.

These rituals and pairings are not merely about the physical consumption of tea; they are a bridge to greater understanding of Chinese philosophy, aesthetics, and the social fabric. Through these practices, tea becomes a vehicle for social interaction, a tool for spiritual meditation, and a profound expression of Chinese cultural identity.

In sum, the world of Chinese tea is a deep reservoir of culture, extending far beyond the simple act of drinking. It involves a sophisticated culinary art, a wide array of rituals that speak to the philosophical and spiritual leanings of Chinese society, and a communal activity that strengthens bonds and fosters peace. In this exploration of tea pairings and rituals, we not only learn about tea as a beverage but also gain insight into a culture that has revered and perfected it for centuries.

2.3 DIM SUM AND STREET FOOD

Delve into the bustling streets and lively tea houses of China, and you will discover a world where the art of dim sum and the vibrancy of street food paint a vivid picture of Chinese culinary traditions. Dim sum, which translates to "touch the heart," does just that with its delightful array of bite-sized dishes, from steamed buns to delicate dumplings. Originating from the Cantonese regions, this culinary practice has evolved into a dining experience that brings families and friends together around the table, sharing and savoring in harmony.

Street food, on the other hand, offers a different kind of communal joy. It captures the essence of everyday life and the ingenuity of vendors who concoct savory snacks and sweet treats from mobile carts and bustling market stalls. Each region boasts its specialties, reflecting local flavors, ingredients, and the rhythms of daily life.

This sub-chapter explores the intricate dance between the refined world of dim sum and the spirited, spontaneous culture of street food. Both serve not only to satisfy hunger but also to foster social connections, celebrate the community, and carry forward the rich tapestry of traditions that define the culinary landscape of China.

2.3.1 HISTORY OF DIM SUM

Dim sum, the quintessential Chinese brunch that combines a variety of flavors and textures in small, bite-sized portions, has a history as rich and diverse as the dishes it comprises. This culinary tradition, deeply rooted in the Cantonese culture of southern China, particularly Guangdong province and Hong Kong, has evolved from humble beginnings to become a global phenomenon, cherished not just for its taste but also for its unique dining experience. The origins of dim sum are intertwined with the history of tea and the development of tea houses along the ancient Silk Road. Travelers on this arduous journey needed places to rest and refresh themselves. Tea houses sprang up along the roadside to serve these weary travelers and rural farmers. It was discovered that tea aids digestion, so tea house proprietors began offering bite-sized snacks as accompaniments, which helped to increase tea sales. This practice laid the groundwork for what would become the dim sum dining experience.

Traditionally, dim sum was consumed within tea gardens, lush spaces where the Chinese elite could enjoy nature while sipping tea, a privilege that was eventually extended to the masses. As these tea gardens evolved into tea houses, the variety of snacks increased, and the tradition of 'yum cha'—drinking tea—became synonymous with enjoying dim sum.

Dim sum's development is marked by its variety and the skill involved in its preparation. Originally, the term "dim sum" literally means "to touch your heart," indicating that these dishes were meant to delight and not to satiate hunger. Over time, the culinary techniques employed became more sophisticated, with an emphasis on flavor, aroma, and presentation. The art of dim sum making became highly respected, involving skills that chefs would pass down through generations.

The repertoire of dim sum is vast, featuring steamed buns like char siu bao (barbecue pork buns), dumplings such as har gow (shrimp dumplings), and siu mai (open-topped pork and shrimp dumplings), along with rice noodle rolls and desserts like egg tarts. Each type of dim sum involves a unique method of preparation, whether steaming, frying, baking, or boiling, which reflects the diverse techniques mastered by dim sum chefs.

The act of enjoying dim sum is also uniquely communal. Diners typically gather around a round table, sharing a variety of dishes that are chosen from roaming carts stacked with bamboo steamers. This method of service, known as 'dim sum cart style,' became popular in Hong Kong and later spread to other parts of the world. The shared experience of choosing dishes as they appear at the table adds an element of surprise and communal decision-making, enhancing the social interaction that is central to the dim sum experience.

Moreover, dim sum dining is not confined to a specific time of day; while traditionally enjoyed in the morning or early afternoon, modern lifestyles have led to its consumption at all times of the day. This flexibility has helped dim sum adapt to various global cultures, contributing to its worldwide popularity.

Today, dim sum holds a place of cultural significance not only in China but across the globe. It embodies the Chinese culinary philosophy of balance and variety, offering a little something for everyone. Restaurants around the world now celebrate the art of dim sum, from high-end establishments to local eateries, ensuring that this culinary tradition continues to evolve while still paying homage to its rich historical roots.

The history of dim sum is a testament to the dynamic nature of culinary traditions, illustrating how food can travel and transform, touching hearts and delighting palates far beyond its original home. As it continues to evolve, dim sum remains a beloved emblem of Chinese hospitality and culinary artistry, a small bite that encapsulates the spirit of a vast culture.

The vibrant street food culture of China is a vivid tapestry that displays the country's rich culinary diversity, each region offering its own unique flavors and specialties. From bustling metropolises like Beijing and Shanghai to the colorful lanes of Chengdu and beyond, the streets are lined with vendors who serve up a variety of dishes that are as rich in flavor as they are in history.

Chinese street food is deeply rooted in the daily lives of its people, offering an accessible, affordable taste of comfort and tradition. These humble eats not only cater to the pace of everyday life but also reflect the local agriculture, regional tastes, and historical influences that shape each area's culinary identity.

One cannot discuss Chinese street food without mentioning the jianbing, a popular breakfast item akin to a crepe, found in the northern regions. Made from a batter of wheat and grain flour, it is cooked on a hot griddle, topped with egg, green onions, hoisin sauce, and crispy wonton crackers, then folded and served hot. This dish's popularity underscores the Chinese penchant for starting the day with warm, freshly prepared food, even when on the go.

Moving south, the street food scene shifts flavors, exemplified by the spicy skewers of meat found in cities like Chongqing and Chengdu. Here, food stalls churn out sticks of seasoned beef, lamb, and vegetables coated in mouth-numbing Sichuan peppercorn mixtures. These spicy treats are a testament to the region's love for bold flavors and a glimpse into the historical spice trade that greatly influenced Sichuanese cuisine.

In coastal regions such as Guangzhou and Hong Kong, seafood plays a significant role in street food offerings. Stalls display tanks of live fish, shrimp, and even exotic seafood, which are cooked to order. This practice is not only a testament to the freshness of the food but also illustrates the Cantonese commitment to quality and flavor, which is paramount in their culinary tradition.

The streets of Shanghai offer another dimension to China's street food tapestry with their shengjianbao—pan-fried pork buns that are a staple of the local diet. The buns are filled with juicy pork and gelatin that melts into broth during cooking, then pan-fried to create a crispy bottom layer, combining textures and flavors in each bite.

Amid these regional specialties, common elements thread through the street food culture, including the emphasis on freshness and quick preparation. Many foods are made to order in front of the customer, creating a performance that enhances the eating experience. This method not only assures the food's freshness but also builds a connection between the vendor and the consumer, a relationship valued in Chinese market culture.

Moreover, street food markets in China are not just about food; they are vibrant social hubs where people from all walks of life gather. These markets are often noisy, lively places where friends meet after work, families enjoy a night out, and young couples share their first dates. In this way, street food does more than satisfy hunger—it fosters community and connection among those who share in its flavors.

However, the rise of urban development and concerns about hygiene and health regulations have posed challenges to street vendors. In recent years, many cities have started to regulate street food more strictly, leading to a decline in traditional street-side dining options. Despite these challenges, the culture persists, adapting to new regulations by shifting into food courts and sanitized food streets where vendors can continue to offer their dishes in a more controlled environment.

This evolution of street food from roadside carts to organized food markets reflects the dynamic nature of this culinary tradition. It shows the resilience of street food culture in adapting to modern changes while continuing to play a crucial role in the culinary life of China. Through these transformations, Chinese street food remains a beloved part of the nation's heritage, offering a delicious lens into the soul of its cities and the histories they carry. As this tradition continues, it remains a vibrant, evolving portrait of Chinese culture, one delectable dish at a time.

CHAPTER 3: ESSENTIAL EQUIPMENT FOR CHINESE COOKING

3.1 INTRODUCTION TO CHINESE KITCHEN TOOLS

Mastering Chinese cuisine extends beyond the harmony of its flavors and ingredients; it also demands an understanding of the traditional tools that make this culinary art form possible. The Chinese kitchen, with its unique set of implements, is a testament to the cuisine's evolution and its deep-rooted culinary traditions.

From the versatile wok, used for everything from stir-frying to steaming, to the sharp, resilient cleavers that make precision cutting a breeze, each tool plays a crucial role in the preparation of authentic Chinese dishes. These tools are not merely functional; they are extensions of the chef's hands, shaped by centuries of culinary practice and designed to achieve the perfect texture and flavor that Chinese cuisine is renowned for.

This sub-chapter delves into the essential equipment every aspiring chef of Chinese cookery needs to know. It will explore how these tools have been adapted over the centuries and how modern innovations have meshed with traditional practices to meet the demands of contemporary cooking while still respecting ancient techniques. Understanding these tools will not only enhance your cooking but also deepen your appreciation of the cultural and historical significance behind each dish that graces your table.

3.1.1 WOKS AND STIR-FRY PANS

At the heart of every Chinese kitchen, the wok is not just a cooking implement but a symbol of Chinese culinary arts that dates back centuries. This versatile cooking vessel, characterized by its deep, rounded bowl and resilient metal construction, is central to the practice of stir-frying, steaming, pan-frying, deep-frying, poaching, boiling, braising, searing, smoking, and roasting seeds. The wok's genius lies in its design, enabling a variety of cooking techniques essential to Chinese cuisine within one ergonomic tool.

The History and Evolution of the Wok

The wok's origins can be traced back to the Han Dynasty, where it began as a rudimentary tool for drying grain. As it evolved, its use expanded beyond simple grain drying to become the staple cooking instrument of Chinese cuisine. This was due to the wok's efficient design, which distributes heat evenly and requires less oil and energy than flat pans, making it ideal for quick cooking methods like stir-frying.

Traditionally made from cast iron or carbon steel, the wok was crafted to withstand high heat while offering a naturally non-stick surface when properly seasoned. Its curved interior allows for easy movement of ingredients, which is essential in stir-frying to achieve the 'wok hei'—literally "wok's air," the subtle, smoky flavor produced by a well-heated wok.

The Art of Stir-Frying

Stir-frying, a technique synonymous with Chinese cooking, is unimaginable without the wok. This method involves cooking food rapidly over high heat while continuously stirring in a circular motion. The shape of the wok allows ingredients to sear quickly when in contact with the bottom and then be tossed up the sides, slowing the cooking process slightly and allowing precise control over the temperature. This technique not only preserves the texture and nutrients of the food but also layers flavors, creating complex dishes from simple ingredients.

Choosing and Caring for a Wok

Selecting the right wok is crucial to mastering Chinese stir-frying. A traditional carbon steel wok is preferred for its quick conduction of heat and durability. New woks require seasoning, a process that involves coating the wok in a layer of oil and heating it to create a protective patina that prevents rusting and sticking. Proper maintenance of a wok involves cleaning it without soap after each use, drying it thoroughly on the stove, and applying a small amount of oil to protect the surface.

Stir-Fry Pans: Modern Adaptations

In modern kitchens, especially in the West, the traditional wok has been adapted into various forms, including flat-bottomed woks and stir-fry pans. These adaptations are designed to accommodate Western stoves, which generally have less intense heat output than Chinese stoves. Stir-fry pans, typically with a flat bottom and a single long handle as opposed to the wok's two shorter handles, offer a similar curvature but are more stable on a standard stove. While these pans do not offer the same depth as traditional woks, they still allow for effective stir-frying by facilitating good contact with the heat source.

The Wok Beyond Stir-Frying

Beyond stir-frying, the wok is incredibly versatile. It is used for steaming (with the addition of a bamboo steamer), smoking meats and fish, and deep-frying. In each use, the wok's shape and material properties offer benefits that other types of cookware cannot match. For deep-frying, for example, the wok's wide opening and deep center allow for frying large amounts of food with less oil than a standard pot.

The wok exemplifies the philosophy of Chinese cooking: versatility, efficiency, and the elevation of simple ingredients into nourishing, flavorful meals. Understanding the wok's capabilities and history not only enhances one's cooking skills but also deepens appreciation for the traditions and techniques that have shaped Chinese cuisine across millennia. In the dance of smoke and fire, the wok is not merely a tool but a bridge to the past, carrying the flavors and wisdom of generations into the dishes it helps create.

3.1.2 CLEAVERS AND KNIVES

In the pantheon of Chinese kitchen essentials, the cleaver stands out as much more than just a simple cutting tool. It is an emblem of Chinese cooking tradition, skillfully used by chefs to chop, slice, dice, and even crush ingredients, embodying the precision and versatility demanded in Chinese cuisine. Alongside the cleaver, various specialized knives also play crucial roles, each designed to perfect specific tasks in the preparation of traditional dishes.

The Chinese Cleaver: A Multifunctional Marvel

At first glance, the Chinese cleaver might look intimidating with its broad blade and sturdy handle, but it is renowned for its remarkable versatility. Unlike Western knives, which often come in sets designated for different purposes, the Chinese cleaver does nearly everything in the kitchen—from butchering meat to julienning delicate vegetables. Its design is a testament to the efficiency valued in Chinese kitchens, where a single tool is expected to perform multiple tasks adeptly.

The cleaver's blade, typically made from carbon steel for durability and a sharp, long-lasting edge, ranges from light to heavy. The lighter cleavers are adept at slicing vegetables and boneless meat, making them a favorite for everyday cooking tasks. The heavier varieties, on the other hand, can handle more demanding jobs like cutting through bones. Using a cleaver effectively requires skill and practice. The broad side of the blade is perfect for smashing garlic and ginger, while its sharp edge can be used for intricate cutting tasks. The technique involves a rhythmic motion where the blade meets the cutting board at a precise angle, controlled entirely by the chef's dexterous hand. This method showcases not only the functional breadth of the cleaver but also the chef's mastery over his tools.

Specialized Chinese Knives

While the cleaver is undoubtedly the centerpiece of Chinese kitchen tools, other specialized knives also find their place. For example, the *Peking Duck* knife is specially designed for slicing the crispy, roasted duck into thin, precise pieces—a key aspect of serving this iconic dish correctly.

Another specialized tool is the *fish knife*, uniquely shaped to handle the delicate flesh of fish. Its design allows chefs to fillet with precision, ensuring that the texture and integrity of the fish are preserved during preparation. This is crucial in Chinese cuisine, where the presentation and quality of ingredients are held in high regard.

Care and Maintenance

The care of Chinese cleavers and knives involves more than just proper cleaning after use. Seasoning the blade, much like seasoning a wok, is crucial in maintaining its longevity and functionality. This process involves oiling the blade to prevent rust and corrosion, especially important for carbon steel tools, which can oxidize if not properly maintained. Sharpening is another critical aspect of care. A well-maintained cleaver or knife is sharpened regularly to ensure that it performs at its best. Traditional methods include using a whetstone, which allows for precise control over the blade's edge. The art of sharpening is often considered as essential as the skills needed to use the tools effectively, with chefs priding themselves on their ability to keep their blades in top condition.

Cultural Significance

Beyond their practical applications, Chinese cleavers and knives carry cultural significance, representing the deep historical roots and the culinary expertise passed down through generations. They are not merely tools but symbols of the culinary heritage that has shaped Chinese cooking practices. In many ways, they are as integral to the identity of Chinese cuisine as the dishes they help create.

In the dance of slicing and dicing, each movement of the cleaver or knife tells a story of tradition, precision, and culinary excellence. These tools are extensions of the chef's hands, translating years of practice and cultural history into the flavors that define Chinese cuisine. As such, understanding and respecting these tools is essential for anyone looking to delve deeper into the rich tapestry of Chinese culinary arts.

3.2 COOKING UTENSILS AND ACCESSORIES

In the symphony of Chinese cooking, each utensil plays a critical role, much like an instrument in an orchestra. Beyond the essential woks and knives, a myriad of specialized cooking utensils and accessories are integral to mastering the art of Chinese cuisine. These tools, from bamboo steamers to spider skimmers, not only facilitate the cooking process but also embody the cultural ingenuity and culinary precision that Chinese cooking demands.

This sub-chapter explores the diverse array of utensils that populate the Chinese kitchen, each tailored to specific tasks that collectively contribute to the effortless execution of complex dishes. Bamboo steamers, for instance, showcase the emphasis on preserving nutrients and textures, offering a gentle cooking method that is perfect for everything from vegetables to dumplings. Similarly, long chopsticks, different from those used at the dining table, allow chefs to manipulate food at a safe distance from the intense heat of the wok.

Understanding these tools is not merely about technical necessity; it is about connecting with the traditions and methods that have been refined over centuries. Each utensil tells a story of regional adaptations and innovations that have shaped the culinary landscape of China, making the act of cooking as much about cultural expression as it is about nourishment.

In the world of Chinese culinary arts, the bamboo steamer stands out as a paragon of both functionality and aesthetic simplicity. These steamers are more than just cooking tools; they are a testament to the age-old Chinese philosophy that emphasizes health, efficiency, and the gentle handling of food. Crafted from bamboo, a material chosen for its durability and sustainability, these steamers allow food to be cooked quickly and without losing nutrients to water or oil, making it an indispensable tool in the health-conscious Chinese kitchen.

Historical and Cultural Significance

The bamboo steamer's history dates back thousands of years, its invention rooted in the need for cooking methods that could retain the texture, color, and nutrients of food. Over the centuries, it has become a symbol of Chinese ingenuity, particularly in the way it seamlessly fits into the tiered layers of a wok—the traditional stove-top tool— allowing for simultaneous cooking of multiple dishes while conserving energy. This method of steaming has not only influenced Chinese cooking but has also been adopted worldwide, appreciated for its straightforward yet effective approach to healthful cooking.

Design and Functionality

Typically, a bamboo steamer consists of one or more tiers stacked atop each other with a lid on top. Each tier can be filled with dishes from dumplings to vegetables, poultry, and seafood. The design allows steam to circulate efficiently, cooking each dish evenly while allowing different flavors to remain distinct and separate. The permeable bamboo layers absorb excess moisture, preventing condensation from dripping onto the food, thus maintaining the desired textures and enhancing subtle flavors.

Culinary Uses and Techniques

The versatility of the bamboo steamer is evident in its ability to prepare a vast array of dishes. Dim sum, for example, one of the hallmarks of Cantonese cuisine, is traditionally served in bamboo steamers. These small, flavorful bite-sized servings are not only a treat to the palate but also a visual delight, often enjoyed as part of a leisurely brunch known as 'yum cha'. Beyond dim sum, bamboo steamers are perfect for cooking rice, fish, and even sponge cakes, each dish benefiting from the gentle cooking process that locks in flavor without adding fat.

Steaming with bamboo is a delicate process that begins with boiling water in a wok or a pot and then placing the steamer above it. The food inside is cooked solely by the rising steam, a method that requires precise timing and temperature control to achieve the perfect texture and degree of doneness. This technique underscores the Chinese culinary emphasis on not just the taste but also the tactile experience of food, ensuring each steamed dish is as pleasing to touch and eat as it is to behold.

Modern Adaptations and Global Influence

While traditional in nature, bamboo steamers have adapted over time to fit modern culinary needs. Innovations include stackable layers added to accommodate the demands of busy restaurants and larger family meals, as well as adaptations that allow steamers to be used in conjunction with modern electric and induction cooktops.

Globally, the bamboo steamer has become a favorite among chefs and home cooks outside China, embraced for its eco-friendliness and effectiveness. It represents a culinary bridge between cultures, a way to share China's rich culinary heritage with the world, providing a window into the values of simplicity, health, and harmony that Chinese cuisine promotes.

Conclusion

The bamboo steamer is not just a tool but a cultural icon, encapsulating the essence of Chinese cooking philosophy. It is a testament to the tradition of innovation and respect for food that is central to Chinese cuisine. As such, understanding and using a bamboo steamer opens up not only a range of culinary possibilities but also an appreciation for a cooking method that is sustainable, healthy, and deeply rooted in one of the world's richest food cultures. With each use, it invites cooks everywhere to partake in a practice that is as ancient as it is relevant, continuing to influence food culture around the globe.

3.2.2 CHINESE SPIDER SKIMMERS

In the bustling kitchens of China, amidst the sizzle of woks and the aromatic mélange of spices, the Chinese spider skimmer emerges as an unsung hero. This quintessential tool, characterized by its long bamboo handle and a wire mesh basket, is indispensable for a variety of cooking tasks, primarily deep-frying and boiling. As modest as it may appear, the spider skimmer is integral to achieving the crispy, delicate textures that Chinese cuisine is celebrated for.

Historical Roots and Design Evolution

The origins of the spider skimmer trace back to ancient Chinese cooking practices, where the need for safely scooping foods from hot liquids was met with ingenuity. Originally crafted from woven bamboo, modern iterations of the skimmer feature a wire mesh attached to a long handle—often made of bamboo or stainless steel—designed to withstand high temperatures while preventing heat transfer, thus allowing chefs to handle the tool comfortably over hot cookware.

The Utility of the Spider Skimmer in Chinese Cooking

The primary use of the spider skimmer is in the deep-frying process. In Chinese cuisine, the texture of deep-fried foods is not merely about the crunch; it's about achieving a balance where the exterior is crisp yet not greasy, and the interior remains succulent. The spider skimmer excels here, allowing cooks to quickly and safely remove items from hot oil at precisely the right moment, ensuring optimal texture without excess oiliness. This tool's fine mesh is perfect for catching even the smallest bits of food, which helps maintain the cleanliness and quality of the frying oil.

In addition to deep-frying, the spider skimmer is essential for blanching—a technique used to prepare ingredients for further cooking or as a finishing touch. Vegetables and meats are often blanched in boiling water and swiftly removed before they overcook, preserving their texture and color. Here, the spider skimmer ensures that ingredients can be quickly and efficiently removed from boiling water, retaining their nutritional quality and aesthetic appeal.

Beyond Functionality: The Spider Skimmer's Role in Culinary Artistry

While the spider skimmer's functionality is undeniable, its value in Chinese culinary tradition extends to the art of presentation. For instance, in the preparation of noodle dishes, where individual ingredients must be cooked precisely and presented attractively, the skimmer allows chefs to assemble dishes layer by layer, maintaining the integrity of each component.

Similarly, in the making of delicate soups and broths, the spider skimmer is used to skim off impurities that rise to the surface, clarifying the liquid to create a pristine base that enhances the soup's flavor and presentation. This aspect of food preparation highlights the meticulous attention to detail that Chinese cuisine demands, where even the simplest dishes are a reflection of craftsmanship.

The Spider Skimmer in Modern and Global Kitchens

As Chinese cuisine has traveled globally, so too has the appreciation for its tools. The spider skimmer has found a place in Western kitchens, where its effectiveness in tasks like poaching eggs, skimming stocks, and frying has been embraced. The adaptation of this tool beyond its traditional context is a testament to its versatility and efficiency.

Moreover, the use of the spider skimmer in professional kitchens around the world underscores a broader culinary dialogue—one that respects traditional techniques while innovating upon them. In this exchange, the spider skimmer is more than just a tool; it is a bridge between cultures, enhancing cooking experiences and culinary outcomes across borders.

Conclusion

The Chinese spider skimmer, with its simple design and multifunctional capabilities, is emblematic of the philosophy that underpins Chinese cooking: that the best culinary tools are those that enhance natural flavors, preserve ingredient integrity, and facilitate precision in cooking. In the dance of flames and flavors that is Chinese cooking, the spider skimmer plays a crucial role, deftly handling ingredients to achieve dishes that are as visually appealing as they are delicious. As such, this tool is not merely a kitchen implement but a vessel of cultural and culinary heritage, pivotal in the hands of those who wield it.

3.3 TIPS FOR SETTING UP YOUR CHINESE KITCHEN

Setting up a Chinese kitchen requires more than just stocking up on ingredients and equipment; it's about creating a space where the rich traditions of Chinese culinary arts can flourish. Whether you are a seasoned chef or a passionate home cook, organizing your kitchen in a way that aligns with the practices of Chinese cooking will enhance both the efficiency of your preparation and the authenticity of the dishes you create.

In this sub-chapter, we will explore essential tips for arranging your Chinese kitchen, focusing on the placement of tools and the organization of ingredients. Key elements such as the strategic positioning of the wok station, optimal storage for perishables, and the organization of spices and seasonings will be addressed. These considerations ensure that everything you need is accessible and that the kitchen supports the dynamic cooking methods characteristic of Chinese cuisine.

Moreover, we will delve into the nuances of integrating modern appliances with traditional tools, such as how to adapt the use of electric ranges for wok cooking or incorporating high-tech steamers without losing the essence of traditional steaming techniques. This guidance will empower you to prepare authentic Chinese meals efficiently and gracefully, turning your kitchen into a haven of culinary excellence where every meal is a testament to the rich heritage of Chinese cooking.

3.3.1 ORGANIZING INGREDIENTS AND UTENSILS

Creating an efficient and functional Chinese kitchen involves thoughtful organization of both ingredients and utensils, reflecting the needs of a cuisine known for its diverse techniques and fast cooking times. The proper arrangement not only saves time but also enhances the culinary experience, allowing the cook to focus on the art of flavor and balance inherent to Chinese cooking.

Strategic Placement of Ingredients

In a Chinese kitchen, accessibility to ingredients is crucial due to the fast-paced nature of many cooking techniques, such as stir-frying. Start by organizing your ingredients based on their frequency of use. Essential spices such as Sichuan peppercorns, star anise, and cloves, along with sauces like soy, oyster, and hoisin, should be within easy reach of the cooking area. Consider using a turntable or tiered spice rack placed near the stove to make the most efficient use of space.

Dry goods like rice, noodles, and dried mushrooms or shrimp can be stored further from the stove but should still be organized for quick access. Use clear, airtight containers to store these items. Not only do these containers keep ingredients fresh, but they also allow you to see what you have at a glance, preventing overbuying and waste.

For perishables, proper refrigeration is key. Vegetables and herbs should be stored in different compartments to avoid cross-contamination and to maintain freshness. Meats and seafood should be kept on lower shelves or drawers, ideally in separate bins, to minimize the risk of drips contaminating other foods.

Utensil Organization

When it comes to utensils, the traditional Chinese kitchen emphasizes simplicity and functionality. The wok is the centerpiece, used for a variety of cooking methods. Store it on an easily accessible hook or a dedicated spot on the stove. Alongside the wok, have a container for essential cooking tools like the Chinese spatula, ladle, and skimmer, which are used frequently and need to be at hand.

Other specialized tools, such as bamboo steamers, dumpling molds, and noodle cutters, should be stored together but out of the primary cooking area to avoid clutter. These can be placed on higher shelves or in cabinets further from the stove, as they are typically used less frequently.

Maximizing Space and Efficiency

In many Chinese kitchens, space is at a premium. Utilizing vertical space can dramatically increase your storage capacity. Install shelves or hanging racks above the counter to store pots, pans, and other large items. Use magnetic strips to safely hang knives in an accessible but secure manner.

Additionally, consider the workflow of your kitchen. Position ingredients and tools in a way that follows the typical sequence of meal preparation — from washing and chopping at the sink to seasoning and cooking at the stove. This setup minimizes unnecessary movement, making the cooking process smoother and faster.

Incorporating Modern and Traditional Elements

While traditional tools and methods are revered, modern Chinese kitchens often blend these with contemporary conveniences. For instance, electric rice cookers and modern steam ovens can sit alongside traditional bamboo steamers, each serving unique purposes. When integrating modern appliances, ensure they do not disrupt the workflow or take away from the accessibility of traditional tools.

Reflecting Cultural Aesthetics

Finally, the organization of a Chinese kitchen is not only about functionality but also about aesthetics and respect for culinary traditions. The arrangement should reflect the elegance and philosophical principles of Chinese culture, which values harmony, order, and balance. Let your kitchen space be a place where these elements coalesce, creating an environment that inspires culinary creativity and celebrates the rich heritage of Chinese cuisine.

Organizing a Chinese kitchen effectively involves more than just placing utensils and ingredients; it's about creating a harmonious environment that respects the fast, flavorful, and health-conscious principles of Chinese cooking. With a well-planned kitchen setup, the act of cooking itself becomes easier, more enjoyable, and deeply intertwined with the cultural and historical significance of the cuisine.

3.3.2 CREATING A FUNCTIONAL COOKING SPACE

Creating a functional cooking space in a Chinese kitchen is about more than just aesthetics; it's about designing an environment that caters to the dynamic and often fast-paced cooking styles that define Chinese cuisine. This space must facilitate efficiency, safety, and culinary creativity, allowing both novice cooks and seasoned chefs to excel in their culinary pursuits.

Design Principles for a Functional Chinese Kitchen

The layout of a Chinese kitchen should revolve around the concept of workflow efficiency. This involves considering the sequence of tasks from preparation to cooking to serving. Ideally, the kitchen layout will follow a triangular path between the stove, sink, and refrigerator, known as the kitchen work triangle. This setup minimizes unnecessary movements and allows for a smoother transition between tasks.

Centralizing the Wok Station

At the heart of the Chinese kitchen is the wok station. This area should be equipped with a high-powered burner that can provide the intense heat needed for stir-frying, which is crucial for achieving the authentic textures and flavors of

Chinese cuisine. The surrounding space must be resistant to heat and easy to clean — materials such as stainless steel or tiled surfaces are ideal. Additionally, there should be ample counter space adjacent to the burner to facilitate the quick movement of ingredients from the chopping board to the wok.

Storage Solutions

Effective storage is crucial in a Chinese kitchen due to the variety of utensils, pots, pans, and ingredients such as spices, sauces, and dried goods that must be easily accessible. Installing deep drawers and cabinets near the cooking area can help store these items efficiently. Utilizing drawer organizers and spice racks can also enhance accessibility and prevent clutter. Overhead racks for hanging pots, pans, and frequently used utensils can save space and add convenience.

Preparation Areas

The preparation area is another cornerstone of the Chinese kitchen, where ingredients are washed, chopped, and marinated. This area should have ample counter space, preferably next to the sink for easy cleanup. A large, durable cutting board is essential, along with organizational features for knives and other cutting tools. Materials for countertops should be chosen for durability and ease of cleaning, such as granite or hardened glass.

Incorporating Ventilation

Given the amount of frying and high-heat cooking in Chinese cuisine, adequate ventilation is crucial. A high-capacity range hood can help remove airborne grease, combustion products, fumes, smoke, odors, heat, and steam, thus maintaining a safe and comfortable cooking environment. This not only helps in keeping the kitchen clean but also protects the health of those cooking.

Safety Features

Safety in a Chinese kitchen is paramount, especially with the open flames and high temperatures involved in wok cooking. Non-slip flooring is essential to prevent accidents, especially in an environment prone to spills. Fire extinguishers should be readily accessible, and all electrical outlets must be properly safeguarded against potential exposure to water and heat.

Ergonomic Considerations

Comfort and ergonomics play critical roles in kitchen design. The height of counters should suit the primary user to prevent strain during food preparation and cooking. Similarly, the placement of heavy equipment and frequently used items should be within easy reach to avoid unnecessary bending or stretching.

Integrating Modern Appliances

While traditional techniques and tools are at the core of Chinese cooking, modern appliances can also find their place in the Chinese kitchen without compromising traditional culinary values. Appliances like rice cookers, modern steam ovens, and induction cooktops can coexist with traditional tools like the wok and bamboo steamers, providing convenience and efficiency.

Conclusion

Designing a functional Chinese kitchen is about creating a space that respects the art of Chinese cooking while accommodating the practical needs of the modern cook. It is a blend of tradition and modernity, where every element is purposefully placed to enhance the cooking experience. Through thoughtful design and careful planning, the kitchen becomes not just a place to prepare meals but a sanctuary for culinary expression, reflecting the rich cultural heritage of Chinese cuisine.

CHAPTER 4: CLASSIC CHINESE BREAKFASTS

4.1 CONGEE AND RICE PORRIDGE VARIETIES

Embarking on a culinary adventure into the heart of Chinese cuisine opens a treasure trove of flavors, techniques, and cultural significance. This introduction is your first step into a world where food is not just sustenance but an art form steeped in millennia of tradition. Chinese cuisine, with its diversity and depth, might initially seem daunting to the uninitiated. However, the secrets to mastering its delights are patience and a willingness to explore.

Imagine walking through the bustling markets of Chengdu, where the air is fragrant with the sizzle of Sichuan pepper and the sweet aroma of star anise. Each dish tells a story, not just of the region's abundant resources but also of its people and their history. The profound connection between Chinese society and its food is evident in every bite of tender Peking duck or each slurp of hearty, hand-pulled noodles.

For beginners, the complexities of Chinese cooking techniques can appear as intricate as the brush strokes of traditional Chinese calligraphy. Yet, just as with any art, beginning with the basics lays the foundation for future mastery. Understanding the balance of the five flavors—sweet, sour, salty, bitter, and umami—is essential. These are not just tastes but pathways to experiencing the Chinese way of life.

Moreover, the ingredients used in Chinese cuisine might seem unfamiliar but unlocking their potential is part of the joy. Each ingredient, from the humble soybean to the exotic lotus root, plays a crucial role in crafting dishes that are as nutritious as they are delicious. As you learn to embrace these elements, you'll discover not only the how but also the why behind each technique and recipe.

As we delve deeper into this chapter, remember that Chinese cuisine is a journey. Each meal is an opportunity to travel from the comfort of your kitchen to the ancient cities of China, where every dish is a celebration of life and heritage. So, gather your wok and chopsticks, and prepare to stir-fry, steam, and simmer your way through a culinary landscape that is as varied as it is rich. With each recipe, you will not just learn how to cook; you will learn how to weave the fabric of Chinese culture into your everyday meals.

4.1.1 PLAIN CONGEE (ZHOU)

EIGHT-TREASURE CONGEE (BABAO ZHOU)

Preparation Time: 20 min

Cooking Time: 2 hr

Mode of Cooking: Slow Cooking

Servings: 6

Ingredients: ●½ cup Glutinous rice, rinsed ●¼ cup Millet, rinsed ●¼ cup Red beans, soaked overnight and drained ●¼ cup Mung beans, rinsed ●¼ cup Dried lotus seeds, soaked for 2hr and drained ●¼ cup Dried longan, soaked for 1hr ●8 cups Water ●¼ cup Rock sugar ●1 piece Dried orange peel

Directions: ●Combine all ingredients except rock sugar in a large pot and bring to a boil over high heat ●Reduce heat to low and cover, simmering for about 2 hrs or until all grains and beans are soft ●Add rock sugar, stirring until dissolved, and cook for an additional 10 min •Serve hot or cold, according to preference

Tips: •This congee can be enjoyed as a sweet breakfast or dessert •Leftovers should be stored in the fridge and can be reheated with a little added water for consistency adjustment •Dried dates or goji berries can also be added for extra sweetness and nutritional value

Nutritional Values: Calories: 215, Fat: 0.5g, Carbs: 50g, Protein: 6g, Sugar: 12g

GINGER INFUSED PLAIN CONGEE (ZHOU)

Preparation Time: 15 min
Cooking Time: 1 hr
Mode of Cooking: Simmering
Servings: 4 Serv.
Ingredients: •1 cup Jasmine rice, rinsed •8 cups Water •1 2-inch piece of ginger, peeled and thinly sliced •1 Tbsp salt
Directions: •Combine rice, water, and ginger slices in a large pot and bring to a boil over high heat •Reduce heat to low and simmer, uncovered, stirring occasionally, until the congee is thick and creamy, about 1 hr •Remove from heat and stir in salt before serving

Tips: •Serve with a drizzle of sesame oil and soy sauce for added flavor •A pinch of white pepper can enhance the warmth of the congee •Fresh scallions or coriander leaves are perfect garnishes for a fresh contrast

Nutritional Values: Calories: 200, Fat: 1g, Carbs: 44g, Protein: 4g, Sugar: 0g

CHICKEN GINGER CONGEE

Preparation Time: 10 min
Cooking Time: 1.5 hr
Mode of Cooking: Simmering
Servings: 4
Ingredients: •1 cup Rice, rinsed •10 cups Chicken broth •2 Chicken thighs, skinless and boneless, cut into pieces •2 Tbsp Ginger, minced •1 Tbsp Salt •2 Tbsp Light soy sauce •Green onions, sliced for garnish •Fried garlic, for garnish
Directions: •In a large pot, bring the chicken broth to a boil •Add rice, chicken pieces, ginger, and salt to the broth and return to a boil •Lower the heat to a simmer

and cook, partially covered, for 1.5 hr, stirring occasionally, until the rice has broken down and the congee has thickened •Stir in light soy sauce and adjust seasoning as needed •Garnish with green onions and fried garlic before serving

Tips: •Adding the minced ginger early in the cooking process infuses the congee with a warming flavor •For a richer texture, shred the chicken thighs after cooking and return them to the pot •For additional color and freshness, consider topping with cilantro alongside green onions

Nutritional Values: Calories: 310, Fat: 8g, Carbs: 34g, Protein: 25g, Sugar: 2g

4.1.2 CENTURY EGG CONGEE (PIDAN ZHOU)

CENTURY EGG TOFU CONGEE

Preparation Time: 15 min
Cooking Time: 1 hr
Mode of Cooking: Simmering
Servings: 4
Ingredients: •1 century egg, peeled and chopped •1 cup jasmine rice, rinsed •6 cups chicken broth •1 block silken tofu, diced •2 Tbsp light soy sauce •1 tsp sesame oil •1 green onion, chopped •1 piece ginger, minced •Salt, to taste •White pepper, to taste
Directions: •Bring chicken broth to a boil in a large pot •Add jasmine rice and simmer on low heat, stirring occasionally, until the rice is fully broken down and the congee has thickened, about 1 hr •Stir in light soy sauce, sesame oil, salt, and white pepper •Gently fold in the diced tofu and century egg, heating through for an additional 2 min •Garnish with green onions and a sprinkle of minced ginger before serving

Tips: •Avoid stirring the congee too vigorously to keep the tofu's texture soft •For extra depth, a drizzle of chili oil on top serves beautifully •Century eggs can be found in Asian supermarkets but ensure they are fresh by checking the packaging date

Nutritional Values: Calories: 220, Fat: 4g, Carbs: 35g, Protein: 12g, Sugar: 2g

GINGER AND CENTURY EGG PORRIDGE

Preparation Time: 20 min
Cooking Time: 90 min

Mode of Cooking: Slow Cook

Servings: 6

Ingredients: •1 cup short grain rice •7 cups water •2 century eggs, peeled and quartered •1 Tbsp grated ginger •2 Tbsp scallions, finely chopped •2 tsp salt •1 tsp white pepper •2 Tbsp cilantro, for garnish •1 Tbsp fried shallots, for garnish

Directions: •Combine rice and water in a large pot and bring to a low boil •Reduce heat to low and simmer, uncovered, stirring occasionally, until the porridge is creamy and the rice grains are soft, about 90 min •Stir in grated ginger, salt, and white pepper during the last 10 min of cooking •Before serving, mix in the quartered century eggs gently •Top each serving with chopped scallions, cilantro, and fried shallots

Tips: •Century egg shells may be tough; soak in warm water for easier peeling •Fresh ginger adds a vibrant kick, but adjust according to preference •Fried shallots add a crunch, available at Asian markets or easily made at home

Nutritional Values: Calories: 180, Fat: 2g, Carbs: 38g, Protein: 6g, Sugar: 1g

PORK AND CENTURY EGG CONGEE

Preparation Time: 10 min

Cooking Time: 2 hr

Mode of Cooking: Stewing

Servings: 4

Ingredients: •½ cup long grain rice •6 cups pork stock •1 century egg, diced •100g lean pork, thinly sliced •2 Tbsp soy sauce •1 Tbsp oyster sauce •1 tsp sugar •Salt to taste •White pepper to taste •2 green onions, chopped for garnish

Directions: •In a large pot, combine rice and pork stock, bringing to a boil over high heat then reducing to a simmer •Add soy sauce, oyster sauce, sugar, salt, and white pepper, stirring well •Cover and simmer on very low heat for 2 hr, until congee is thick and creamy •In the last 10 min of cooking, add the thinly sliced pork and diced century egg to the congee, allowing the pork to cook through and the egg to warm •Serve hot, garnished with chopped green onions

Tips: •Pork should be sliced as thinly as possible for quick cooking •A touch of sesame oil can be added before serving for an aromatic finish •Adjust the consistency by adding more pork stock if needed

Nutritional Values: Calories: 240, Fat: 5g, Carbs: 32g, Protein: 15g, Sugar: 2g

4.2 BREAKFAST DUMPLINGS AND BUNS

Dawn in the bustling streets of Shanghai brings with it the comforting aromas of breakfast dumplings and buns, an essential part of Chinese morning rituals. These delectable treats, enjoyed across many regions, embody more than just sustenance; they are a warm, hearty welcome to the new day. Each bun and dumpling is a bite-sized piece of culinary heritage, a soft, steamy embrace of dough filled with meticulously seasoned ingredients.

From the northern lands where wheat dominates, to the rice-rich south, each locale infuses its unique character into these creations. Consider the famed *shengjian bao*, a Shanghai specialty: pan-fried to golden perfection, these soup dumplings offer a crispy bottom that contrasts delightfully with the soft, juicy top. Just as engaging are the fluffy *char siu bao* from Cantonese cuisine, with their sweet and savory barbecued pork filling that melts in your mouth, narrating tales of ancient spice routes and regional culinary evolution.

Preparing these dumplings and buns at home invites a morning filled with the rich scents of steaming bamboo baskets, an act that connects the cook to centuries of tradition. The process, although intricate, is as rewarding as it is educational, offering a window into the discipline and artistry that Chinese cooking demands. As you fold, stuff, and steam, you're not just making breakfast; you're crafting a moment of cultural communion, one delectable bite at a time.

SHENGJIAN MANTOU (PAN-FRIED PORK BUNS)

Preparation Time: 1 hr 30 min

Cooking Time: 10 min

Mode of Cooking: Pan-frying

Servings: 4

Ingredients: ●For the dough: 2 cups all-purpose flour ●¾ cup warm water ●1 tsp active dry yeast ●1 Tbsp sugar ●For the filling: 1 lb ground pork ●2 Tbsp soy sauce ●1 Tbsp sesame oil ●2 tsp sugar ●2 green onions, finely chopped ●1 tsp ginger, minced ●¼ cup chicken stock ●For cooking: 2 Tbsp vegetable oil ●½ cup water ●Sesame seeds for garnish ●Chopped green onion for garnish

Directions: ●Mix flour, sugar, yeast, and water to form a smooth dough ●Let it rest in a warm place until doubled in size, about 1 hr ●Mix ground pork, soy sauce, sesame oil, sugar, green onions, ginger, and chicken stock for the filling ●Divide the dough into small balls and flatten each ●Place a spoonful of filling in the center of each and seal tightly ●Heat oil in a pan, place buns seam side down, cook until bottoms are golden brown ●Add water, cover, and steam until water evaporates ●Garnish with sesame seeds and chopped green onions

Tips: ●Use a rolling pin to evenly flatten the dough balls, ensuring uniform cooking ●Make sure to seal the buns tightly to prevent the filling from leaking out during cooking

Nutritional Values: Calories: 450, Fat: 25g, Carbs: 35g, Protein: 20g, Sugar: 3g

JI DAN BING (CHINESE EGG PANCAKE)

Preparation Time: 15 min

Cooking Time: 5 min

Mode of Cooking: Pan-frying

Servings: 2

Ingredients: ●For the pancake: 1 cup all-purpose flour ●½ cup water ●Pinch of salt ●For the filling: 2 eggs ●2 Tbsp chopped green onions ●1 tsp sesame oil ●To serve: Hoisin sauce ●Sriracha sauce ●Soy sauce

Directions: ●Combine flour, water, and salt to make a smooth, elastic dough ●Roll out into thin pancakes ●Heat a non-stick pan over medium heat, place pancake dough in the pan ●Crack an egg over the pancake, spreading the egg evenly with a spatula ●Sprinkle chopped green onions and drizzle sesame oil over the egg ●Once the egg is set, fold the pancake in half and remove from pan ●Serve with hoisin sauce, sriracha, and soy sauce for dipping

Tips: ●The thinner the pancake, the crispier it will be ●Avoid overcooking the egg to maintain a slightly runny yolk for a rich flavor

Nutritional Values: Calories: 320, Fat: 10g, Carbs: 45g, Protein: 13g, Sugar: 2g

LUO BO SI BING (RADISH STRIPS PANCAKE)

Preparation Time: 40 min

Cooking Time: 10 min

Mode of Cooking: Pan-frying

Servings: 3

Ingredients: ●2 cups all-purpose flour ●1 cup grated daikon radish ●½ cup water ●2 green onions, finely chopped ●1 Tbsp soy sauce ●1 tsp sesame oil ●Salt and pepper to taste ●Vegetable oil for frying

Directions: ●Mix flour and water to form a soft dough, let it rest for 30 min ●Squeeze excess moisture from grated radish ●Mix radish, green onions, soy sauce, sesame oil, salt, and pepper ●Divide dough into small portions, roll out each into a thin circle ●Spread radish mixture on half of the dough circle, fold over and seal edges ●Heat oil in a pan, fry each pancake until golden brown on both sides, turning once

Tips: •Serve hot with a side of soy sauce or chili oil for dipping •Squeezing out moisture from radish ensures the pancake isn't soggy

Nutritional Values: Calories: 290, Fat: 10g, Carbs: 42g, Protein: 6g, Sugar: 2g

4.2.2 CHAR SIU BAO (STEAMED BBQ PORK BUNS)

TRADITIONAL CHAR SIU BAO (STEAMED BBQ PORK BUNS)

Preparation Time: 2 hrs

Cooking Time: 20 min

Mode of Cooking: Steaming

Servings: 12

Ingredients: •For the Dough: 500g plain flour •1 Tbsp sugar •1 Tbsp yeast •300ml warm water •1 Tsp baking powder •For the Filling: 300g char siu pork, finely chopped •2 Tbsp oyster sauce •1 Tbsp soy sauce •1 Tbsp sesame oil •1 Tbsp sugar •2 Tbsp cornstarch mixed with 4 Tbsp water •1 Tbsp vegetable oil •2 green onions, chopped •1 clove garlic, minced

Directions: •Prepare the dough: Dissolve sugar and yeast in warm water and set aside for 5 min until frothy •Mix flour and baking powder in a large bowl •Make a well in the center and pour in the yeast mixture •Mix until a soft dough forms, then knead on a floured surface for about 10 min until smooth •Place in a greased bowl, cover with a damp cloth, and let rise in a warm place for 1 hr until doubled in size •Meanwhile, prepare the filling: Heat vegetable oil in a saucepan over medium heat •Sauté garlic and green onions until fragrant •Add chopped char siu pork, oyster sauce, soy sauce, sesame oil, and sugar •Cook for 2-3 min, then stir in the cornstarch mixture until the sauce thickens •Set aside to cool •Punch down the dough and divide into 12 equal pieces •Roll each piece into a ball, then flatten into a disc •Spoon a portion of the filling into the center of each disc •Gather the edges together and twist to seal •Place each bun on a small piece of parchment paper •Arrange buns in a steamer, leaving space between each •Cover and let rise for another 30 min •Steam buns over boiling water for 20 min•Remove from steamer and serve hot

Tips: •Use a thermometer to ensure the water is at the correct temperature for activating the yeast •Apply a light layer of oil on the surface of the buns before steaming to prevent them from drying out •If the dough is too sticky, add a little more flour until it becomes manageable but still soft

Nutritional Values: Calories: 220, Fat: 3g, Carbs: 40g, Protein: 9g, Sugar: 5g

GOLDEN CUSTARD BUNS (LIU SHA BAO)

Preparation Time: 20 min

Cooking Time: 15 min

Mode of Cooking: Steaming

Servings: 10

Ingredients: •For the dough: 2 C. all-purpose flour •1 Tbsp sugar •1 Tsp yeast •¾ C. warm water •For the custard filling: 4 egg yolks •½ C. sugar •3 Tbsp cornstarch •1 C. milk •2 Tbsp butter •¼ tsp salt •1 Tsp vanilla extract

Directions: •Prepare the custard filling by whisking together egg yolks and sugar until smooth •In a separate bowl, dissolve cornstarch in a small amount of milk, then add to the egg mixture along with the rest of the milk and cook over medium heat, stirring constantly until thickened •Remove from heat, stir in butter, salt, and vanilla extract, and let cool completely •For the dough, mix flour, sugar, and yeast in a bowl, then gradually add warm water to form a soft dough •Knead the dough until smooth, cover, and let rise until doubled in size •Divide the dough and custard into 10 equal portions •Flatten each dough portion and place a spoonful of custard in the center, then wrap and seal •Place the buns on parchment paper, cover, and let rise again for about 20 min •Steam the buns over boiling water for 15 min

Tips: •To achieve a glossy finish, brush the buns with a little oil before steaming •Make sure the custard is completely cool before filling to prevent the dough from becoming soggy

Nutritional Values: Calories: 225, Fat: 7g, Carbs: 35g, Protein: 5g, Sugar: 15g

FIVE SPICE CHICKEN BUNS (WU XIANG JI BAO)

Preparation Time: 35 min

Cooking Time: 20 min

Mode of Cooking: Steaming

Servings: 12

Ingredients: ●For the filling: 2 C. cooked and shredded chicken breast ●1 Tbsp Chinese five spice powder ●2 Tbsp soy sauce ●1 Tbsp oyster sauce ●1 Tsp sesame oil ●2 Tsp sugar ●¼ C. chopped scallions ●For the dough: 2½ C. all-purpose flour ●1 Tbsp sugar ●1 Tsp yeast ●1 C. warm water ●1 Tbsp vegetable oil

Directions: ●Combine shredded chicken, five spice powder, soy sauce, oyster sauce, sesame oil, sugar, and scallions in a bowl and set aside to marinate ●Mix flour, sugar, and yeast in another bowl, then add warm water and vegetable oil to form a soft dough ●Knead until smooth, cover, and let rise until doubled ●Divide the dough into 12 pieces, flatten each piece, and place a portion of the chicken filling in the center ●Gather edges to seal the buns and place them on parchment paper ●Let the buns rise covered for an additional 20 min ●Steam over boiling water for 20 min

Tips: ●Brush buns with a thin coat of vegetable oil after steaming for a sheen finish ●Let the buns cool slightly before serving to allow the filling to set

Nutritional Values: Calories: 210, Fat: 4g, Carbs: 32g, Protein: 12g, Sugar: 3g

4.3 CHINESE PANCAKES AND PASTRIES

Morning in any Chinese kitchen comes alive with the sizzling sounds and irresistible aromas of pancakes and pastries, essential elements of traditional Chinese breakfasts. These staples, each with their distinct textures and flavors, are as varied as the landscapes of China itself. Among the most cherished are the *cong you bing*, or scallion pancakes, whose crispy, flaky layers tell stories of old Beijing's bustling morning markets, where they are often enjoyed fresh off the griddle with a dollop of fragrant soy sauce.

Traveling further south, the sweet red bean paste pancakes, known as *hong dou bing*, offer a different tale. These delights showcase the influence of sweet flavors in southern Chinese cuisine, combining the gentle sweetness of red beans encased in a tender, golden-brown crust, symbolizing comfort and warmth on a brisk morning.

The art of making these pancakes and pastries is a dance of balance and precision, with each ingredient meticulously chosen and each step carefully executed to maintain authenticity and taste. Preparing them requires not just culinary skills but also a connection to the past, as each turn of the spatula or fold of the dough deepens one's appreciation for the rich heritage and craftsmanship that define Chinese gastronomy.

As we explore these recipes, remember that making Chinese pancakes and pastries is more than a morning ritual; it is an invitation to savor history and culture, one delicious bite at a time.

4.3.1 SCALLION PANCAKES (CONG YOU BING)

FIVE-SPICE TOFU PANCAKES

Preparation Time: 20 min

Cooking Time: 10 min

Mode of Cooking: Pan-Frying

Servings: 4

Ingredients: ●1 block firm tofu, drained and mashed ●1½ cups all-purpose flour ●2 Tbsp soy sauce ●1 tsp Chinese five-spice powder ●1 cup chopped kale or bok choy ●½ cup shredded carrots ●2 cloves garlic, minced ●Salt and pepper to taste ●Vegetable oil for frying

Directions: ●In a large bowl, combine the mashed tofu with soy sauce, five-spice powder, chopped kale or bok choy, shredded carrots, minced garlic, and season with salt and pepper ●Gradually add flour to the mixture until a dough-like consistency is reached ●Shape the dough into small pancakes ●Heat vegetable oil in a skillet over medium heat ●Fry each pancake until golden brown and crispy, about 5 min on each side ●Serve hot, garnished with additional soy sauce if desired

Tips: ●Avoid overworking the dough to keep pancakes tender ●Incorporate vegetables of choice for a custom flavor profile ●Press tofu under a heavy object for 30 minutes prior to use, for better texture
Nutritional Values: Calories: 215, Fat: 9g, Carbs: 27g, Protein: 11g, Sugar: 2g

CLASSIC SCALLION PANCAKES (CONG YOU BING)

Preparation Time: 15 min
Cooking Time: 5 min
Mode of Cooking: Pan-Frying
Servings: 4
Ingredients: ●2 cups all-purpose flour ●¾ cup boiling water ●1 Tbsp sesame oil ●1 cup finely chopped scallions ●Salt to taste ●Vegetable oil for frying
Directions: ●Slowly mix flour with boiling water, stirring continuously until dough forms ●On a floured surface, knead dough until smooth, approximately 5 minutes, then cover with a damp cloth and let it rest for 30 min ●Divide dough into 4 equal parts ●Roll out one part into a thin circle ●Brush sesame oil over the surface, sprinkle with salt and a portion of chopped scallions ●Roll the dough tightly into a log, then coil the log into a round dough ball ●Flatten the dough ball into a pancake, ensuring scallions are evenly distributed ●Heat a pan with vegetable oil over medium heat ●Fry each pancake until golden brown, about 2-3 min on each side ●Drain on paper towels and serve warm
Tips: ●Use a rolling pin for thinner pancakes for a crispier texture ●Keep the rolled dough balls covered to prevent drying out before frying ●For a spicy

variation, add a pinch of crushed red pepper flakes to the scallions
Nutritional Values: Calories: 250, Fat: 10g, Carbs: 34g, Protein: 4g, Sugar: 1g

RED BEAN PASTE PANCAKES

Preparation Time: 20 min
Cooking Time: 5 min
Mode of Cooking: Pan-Frying
Servings: 6
Ingredients: ●1 cup all-purpose flour ●½ cup warm water ●¾ cup red bean paste ●Pinch of salt ●Vegetable oil for frying
Directions: ●Mix all-purpose flour, warm water, and a pinch of salt in a bowl until a smooth dough forms ●Divide the dough into 6 equal portions ●Roll each portion into a ball and flatten into a pancake shape ●Place a spoonful of red bean paste in the center of each pancake, fold the dough to cover the filling, and gently flatten ●Heat vegetable oil in a pan over medium heat ●Fry the pancakes until golden on both sides, approximately 2 min per side ●Serve warm or at room temperature
Tips: ●Do not overfill pancakes to prevent leaking during frying ●For a lighter version, use a non-stick pan with minimal oil ●Experiment with different sweet bean pastes for variety
Nutritional Values: Calories: 180, Fat: 8g, Carbs: 24g, Protein: 3g, Sugar: 10g

4.3.2 RED BEAN PASTE PANCAKES (HONG DOU BING)

JASMINE TEA INFUSED RED BEAN PASTE PANCAKES

Preparation Time: 25 min
Cooking Time: 15 min
Mode of Cooking: Pan-frying
Servings: 6
Ingredients: ●1 cup all-purpose flour ●2 Tbsp sugar ●½ tsp salt ●1 Tbsp baking powder ●⅔ cup milk ●1 egg, beaten ●2 Tbsp unsalted butter, melted ●¾ cup red bean paste ●1 Tbsp jasmine tea leaves, finely ground ●2 Tbsp vegetable oil for frying

Directions: •Combine flour, sugar, salt, and baking powder in a large bowl •In another bowl, mix milk, egg, and melted butter •Gradually add the wet ingredients to the dry, stirring until just combined •Stir in ground jasmine tea leaves •Heat oil in a pan over medium heat •Pour ¼ cup of batter for each pancake, spreading it slightly •Place a tablespoon of red bean paste in the center of each pancake •Cover with another tablespoon of batter •Cook until bubbles form on the surface, then flip and cook until golden brown

Tips: •Serve pancakes warm with a sprinkle of powdered sugar for an extra touch •Use a non-stick pan to prevent sticking and ensure even cooking

Nutritional Values: Calories: 290, Fat: 9g, Carbs: 46g, Protein: 7g, Sugar: 15g

SAVORY FIVE-SPICE RED BEAN PANCAKES

Preparation Time: 30 min
Cooking Time: 20 min
Mode of Cooking: Pan-frying
Servings: 4
Ingredients: •1 cup red bean paste •1½ cups all-purpose flour •1 tsp Chinese five-spice powder •¼ tsp salt •1 cup water •4 green onions, finely chopped •1 red chili, deseeded and finely chopped •4 Tbsp vegetable oil for frying •Soy sauce for dipping
Directions: •In a bowl, combine flour, five-spice powder, and salt •Gradually add water, stirring to form a smooth batter •Stir in chopped green onions and red chili •Let the batter sit for 10 minutes for flavors to meld •Heat oil in a large skillet over medium-high heat •Pour ¼ cup of batter into the skillet, spreading it into a thin circle •Spoon red bean paste over half of the circle, then fold the other half over, pressing down

slightly to seal •Cook until each side is crisp and golden brown, flipping once

Tips: •Serve hot with soy sauce for dipping •Let the batter rest to allow the five-spice flavor to develop fully •Fry pancakes at a consistent medium-high heat for a crisp exterior

Nutritional Values: Calories: 360, Fat: 12g, Carbs: 54g, Protein: 8g, Sugar: 16g

COCONUT AND RED BEAN PASTE CRÊPES

Preparation Time: 15 min
Cooking Time: 10 min
Mode of Cooking: Pan-frying
Servings: 8
Ingredients: •1 cup all-purpose flour •2 eggs •1½ cups coconut milk •Pinch of salt •1 tsp sugar •1 cup red bean paste •1 Tbsp coconut oil, plus extra for frying •Shredded coconut for garnish
Directions: •Whisk together flour, eggs, coconut milk, salt, and sugar until smooth to make the batter •Heat a little coconut oil in a non-stick pan over medium heat •Pour a thin layer of batter, tilting the pan to spread it out into a thin crêpe •Cook until the edges start to lift, then flip and cook the other side until lightly golden •Spread red bean paste over half the crêpe, fold in half, and then fold again to form a quarter circle •Repeat with remaining batter

Tips: •Garnish with shredded coconut before serving •Using coconut milk in the batter adds a subtle sweetness and tropical flavor to complement the red bean paste

Nutritional Values: Calories: 280, Fat: 13g, Carbs: 35g, Protein: 6g, Sugar: 12g

CHAPTER 5: NOODLE DELIGHTS

5.1 HAND-PULLED AND KNIFE-CUT NOODLES

In the world of Chinese noodle making, the crafts of hand-pulling (*la mian*) and knife-cutting (*dao xiao mian*) stand as testaments to the culinary expertise and cultural heritage that have been passed down through generations. These techniques, each with their distinct rhythmic beauty and precision, transform simple dough into spectacular arrays of noodles that are as pleasing to the eye as they are to the palate.

Imagine the skilled hands of a noodle master in Lanzhou, rhythmically stretching and folding the dough, the air punctuated with the thwap of dough hitting the counter, eventually forming perfectly even, gossamer-thin strands. This is *la mian*, a dance of strength and finesse, requiring years to master but only moments to appreciate on the plate. Conversely, *dao xiao mian* offers a different spectacle. Here, the chef uses a sharp knife to shave swift, thick cuts of noodle directly into a boiling pot of water. Originating from the mountains of Shanxi, where the cold climate favored the hearty texture of these noodles, the method showcases a rustic, yet equally sophisticated, approach to noodle making.

Each bowl of noodles, whether silken strands of *la mian* or the chewy ribbons of *dao xiao mian*, tells a story of regional climates, historical necessities, and the unyielding pursuit of culinary perfection. As we delve into the recipes and techniques, these noodles provide not just sustenance, but a connection to the rich tapestry of Chinese culture, inviting you to partake in a centuries-old culinary art that is both a feast for the senses and a bridge to the past.

5.1.1 LANZHOU BEEF NOODLE SOUP

LANZHOU BEEF NOODLE SOUP

Preparation Time: 30 min.
Cooking Time: 2 hrs.
Mode of Cooking: Stovetop
Servings: 4
Ingredients: ●1 lb. beef shank, sliced thinly ●4 qt. water ●2 Tbsp. sunflower oil ●5 slices ginger ●3 cloves garlic, smashed ●2 green onions, chopped ●1 cinnamon stick ●2 star anise ●1 Tbsp. Sichuan peppercorns ●1/4 cup soy sauce ●2 Tbsp. beef bouillon powder ●Hand-pulled wheat noodles, enough for four servings ●Bok choy, quartered, as desired ●1 tsp. white pepper ●Cilantro and sliced green onions, for garnish ●Chili oil, to taste

Directions: ●In a large pot, bring water to a boil and blanch beef shank for 2 min. to remove impurities ●Remove beef and rinse ●Heat oil in the same pot over medium heat ●Sauté ginger, garlic, and green onions until fragrant about 1 min. ●Add beef shank back to the pot with cinnamon stick, star anise, Sichuan peppercorns, soy sauce, beef bouillon, and 4 qt. water or enough to cover ●Bring to a boil, then simmer on low for 1.5 hrs. until beef is tender ●Cook noodles according to package instructions ●Blanch bok choy in boiling water for 2 min. ●To serve, place noodles in bowls, ladle broth and beef over noodles, and add bok choy ●Garnish with cilantro, green onions, white pepper, and chili oil to taste

Tips: ●Use a sieve to rinse blanched beef to ensure clean broth ●Toast spices before adding them to the pot for enhanced flavor ●Adjust chili oil according to spice preference

Nutritional Values: Calories: 420, Fat: 12g, Carbs: 46g, Protein: 32g, Sugar: 3g

XI'AN SPICY CUMIN LAMB NOODLES

Preparation Time: 45 min.

Cooking Time: 1 hr.

Mode of Cooking: Stovetop

Servings: 4

Ingredients: ●1 lb. lamb, thinly sliced ●3 Tbsp. cumin seeds, crushed ●1 tsp. Sichuan peppercorns, crushed ●2 Tbsp. soy sauce ●1 Tbsp. rice vinegar ●1 tsp. cornstarch ●2 Tbsp. vegetable oil ●4 cloves garlic, minced ●1 Tbsp. ginger, minced ●3 green onions, sliced ●1 red bell pepper, julienned ●4 servings hand-pulled noodles ●2 tsp. chili flakes ●Salt and pepper to taste ●Fresh cilantro, for garnish ●Toasted sesame seeds, for garnish

Directions: ●Marinate lamb with cumin, Sichuan peppercorns, soy sauce, rice vinegar, cornstarch, salt, and pepper for 30 min. ●Heat oil in a wok over high heat, stir-fry garlic, ginger, and lamb until lamb is just cooked, about 3-4 min. ●Reduce heat to medium, add green onions and bell pepper, cook until softened ●Cook noodles according to package instructions, drain ●Toss noodles with lamb mixture, season with chili flakes ●Garnish with cilantro and sesame seeds before serving

Tips: ●Marinating the lamb beforehand tenderizes and infuses it with flavor ●Toast cumin and Sichuan peppercorns to release their oils and enhance the dish's aroma ●Add chili flakes according to spice preference

Nutritional Values: Calories: 650, Fat: 28g, Carbs: 62g, Protein: 38g, Sugar: 4g

GUILIN RICE NOODLES WITH BRAISED BEEF

Preparation Time: 20 min.

Cooking Time: 3 hrs.

Mode of Cooking: Stovetop

Servings: 4

Ingredients: ●1 lb. beef brisket, cut into chunks ●5 cups water ●3 star anise ●1 cinnamon stick ●5 slices ginger ●2 Tbsp. soy sauce ●1 Tbsp. oyster sauce ●2 tsp. sugar ●1 Tbsp. rice wine ●4 servings rice noodles ●1/4 lb. bean sprouts ●Fresh herbs (basil, cilantro) ●Pickled mustard greens, chopped ●Peanuts, crushed, for garnish ●Green onions, chopped, for garnish ●Chili oil, to taste

Directions: ●Combine beef, water, star anise, cinnamon, ginger, soy sauce, oyster sauce, sugar, and rice wine in a large pot ●Bring to a boil and then simmer on low heat for 3 hrs. until beef is tender ●Cook rice noodles according to package instructions, drain ●Briefly blanch bean sprouts in boiling water for 30 sec. ●To serve, place noodles in bowls, top with beef, ladle braised broth over, and garnish with fresh herbs, mustard greens, peanuts, green onions, and chili oil

Tips: ●Skimming foam and fat off the top of the broth as it cooks will yield a clearer soup ●Use a strainer to remove spices before serving for a smoother texture ●Adjust the amount of chili oil for desired spiciness

Nutritional Values: Calories: 540, Fat: 14g, Carbs: 68g, Protein: 36g, Sugar: 5g

5.1.2 DAO XIAO MIAN (KNIFE-CUT NOODLES)

TRADITIONAL SHAANXI BIANG BIANG NOODLES

Preparation Time: 40 min

Cooking Time: 20 min

Mode of Cooking: Boiling

Servings: 4

Ingredients: ●For Noodles: 2 cups all-purpose flour ●1 tsp salt ●3/4 cup warm water ●For Topping: 2 Tbsp vegetable oil ●4 garlic cloves, minced ●1 Tbsp Sichuan peppercorns ●2 green onions, chopped ●1/4 cup cilantro, chopped ●4 Tbsp soy sauce ●2 Tbsp Chinkiang vinegar ●1 Tbsp chili oil ●1 tsp sugar

Directions: ●Mix flour and salt in a large bowl, add water gradually while kneading until dough forms; let rest for 30 min, covered ●Roll out the dough into a rectangle, cut into 1-inch wide strips; pull each strip by hand to stretch into a long noodle, slap it against the counter, and then place it in boiling water until cooked through ●Heat oil in a pan, add garlic and Sichuan peppercorns, cook until fragrant; remove from heat, add green onions, cilantro, soy sauce, vinegar, chili oil, and sugar, mix well ●Pour sauce over boiled noodles, toss to combine

Tips: ●Stretch noodles gently to prevent breaking ●Use a slotted spoon to remove noodles from water to avoid breaking ●Adjust chili oil according to spice preference

Nutritional Values: Calories: 320, Fat: 10g, Carbs: 48g, Protein: 8g, Sugar: 2g

DAO XIAO MIAN WITH PORK AND BOK CHOY

Preparation Time: 1 hr
Cooking Time: 30 min
Mode of Cooking: Boiling and Stir-Frying
Servings: 4
Ingredients: ●For Noodles: 2 cups all-purpose flour ●1/2 tsp salt ●2/3 cup water ●For Stir-Fry: 1 lb pork shoulder, thinly sliced ●2 Tbsp soy sauce ●1 Tbsp Shaoxing wine ●2 tsp sugar ●2 Tbsp vegetable oil ●1 Tbsp ginger, minced ●2 cups bok choy, chopped ●2 cloves garlic, minced ●1/2 cup chicken stock ●salt and pepper to taste

Directions: ●Prepare noodles by mixing flour, salt, and water to form a dough; rest for 40 min ●Using a sharp knife, slice dough into thin noodles directly into boiling water; cook until noodle floats to the surface, then drain ●Marinate pork with soy sauce, Shaoxing wine, and sugar for 20 min ●Heat oil in a pan over high heat, add pork, cook until browned; remove pork from pan ●In the same pan, add ginger, garlic, and bok choy, stir-fry until bok choy is wilted ●Add cooked pork, noodles, and chicken stock to the pan; cook until most of the liquid has evaporated

Tips: ●Slice the dough at a 45-degree angle for wider noodles ●Stir-fry on high heat to achieve wok hei, the characteristic smoky flavor of Chinese stir-frying ●Add additional vegetables like shiitake mushrooms or bell peppers for extra crunch

Nutritional Values: Calories: 450, Fat: 20g, Carbs: 40g, Protein: 25g, Sugar: 4g

BEEF SHANK DAO XIAO MIAN

Preparation Time: 30 min
Cooking Time: 2 hr
Mode of Cooking: Stovetop
Servings: 4
Ingredients: ●2 lb. beef shank ●1 Tbsp soy sauce ●2 Tbsp Shaoxing wine ●1-inch ginger, sliced ●3 cloves garlic, minced ●4 cups water ●2 star anise ●1 cinnamon stick ●Salt to taste ●For noodles: 2 cups all-purpose flour ●1/2 tsp salt ●3/4 cup water ●For garnish: 2 green onions, chopped ●1/4 cup cilantro, chopped ●Chili oil to taste

Directions: ●Combine beef shank, soy sauce, Shaoxing wine, ginger, garlic, water, star anise, and cinnamon stick in a pot and bring to a boil. Lower heat and simmer for 2 hr until beef is tender ●Remove beef shank, let cool, then slice thinly ●Mix flour and salt in a bowl, gradually add water while stirring until dough forms. Rest dough for 20 min ●On a floured surface, roll dough into a rectangle, then use a sharp knife to slice into thin noodles ●Bring a large pot of water to boil, cook noodles for about 2 min until tender. Drain ●Serve noodles in bowls, topped with beef shank slices, green onions, cilantro, and a drizzle of chili oil

Tips: ●Use a very sharp knife to slice noodles for uniformity ●Allow the beef shank to cool completely for easier slicing ●Adjust chili oil according to taste for spiciness

Nutritional Values: Calories: 550, Fat: 18g, Carbs: 58g, Protein: 38g, Sugar: 1g

5.2 STIR-FRIED NOODLE DISHES

Stir-fried noodles capture the essence of Chinese cooking—fast, fiery, and brimming with flavor. Each dish, from the famous *chow mein* to the spicy *Singapore noodles*, showcases a mastery of the wok's intense heat and the chef's swift movements. The key lies in the harmony of textures and flavors, achieved through the rapid tossing of fresh ingredients over a scorching flame.

As you step into a Chinese kitchen, the clang of the wok and the roar of the flame become part of the cooking symphony. Ingredients, precut and seasoned, stand ready by the stove, each waiting for its moment in the spotlight. The chef, a conductor of sorts, orchestrates this culinary performance with precision—garlic and onions sizzle first, releasing their pungent aromas, followed by crisp vegetables and tender slices of meat, each adding layers of texture and flavor.

Noodles enter the wok last, soaking up the rich sauces and melding with the other ingredients in a glorious mix. The result is a dish vibrant in color and robust in taste, often enhanced with a hint of smoky sweetness from the wok's seasoned history. This method not only cooks but also carves deep flavors into the noodles, encapsulating a multitude of ingredients in each forkful.

Engaging in the art of stir-frying noodles at home brings not just the flavors of China to your table, but also a piece of its culinary soul, teaching patience, timing, and respect for the ingredients. Each dish you create is a step closer to understanding the dynamic balance of Chinese cuisine.

5.2.1 CHOW MEIN WITH VEGETABLES

CLASSIC VEGETABLE CHOW MEIN

Preparation Time: 15 min
Cooking Time: 15 min
Mode of Cooking: Stir-Frying
Servings: 4
Ingredients: ●2 Tbsp peanut oil ●200g egg noodles ●1 cup sliced napa cabbage ●½ cup shredded carrot ●½ cup sliced bell pepper ●½ cup bean sprouts ●1 sliced green onion ●2 garlic cloves, minced ●1 tsp grated ginger ●3 Tbsp soy sauce ●1 Tbsp oyster sauce ●1 Tbsp sesame oil ●2 tsp sugar
Directions: ●Cook noodles according to package instructions, then rinse under cold water and set aside ●Heat peanut oil in a large wok over high heat and stir-fry garlic and ginger until aromatic ●Add napa cabbage, carrot, bell pepper, and bean sprouts, stirring quickly

to keep the vegetables crisp ●Toss in the noodles, green onion, soy sauce, oyster sauce, sesame oil, and sugar, combining well ●Stir-fry for an additional 3-4 minutes until everything is heated through and coated in sauce

Tips: ●Make sure your wok is extremely hot before adding vegetables to achieve the perfect sear without overcooking ●Slice vegetables thinly for quick and even cooking ●For a gluten-free version, use tamari instead of soy sauce
Nutritional Values: Calories: 280, Fat: 9g, Carbs: 42g, Protein: 8g, Sugar: 5g

SPICY SZECHUAN STYLE NOODLES

Preparation Time: 20 min
Cooking Time: 10 min
Mode of Cooking: Boiling and Stir-Frying
Servings: 2
Ingredients: ●150g dried wheat noodles ●2 Tbsp vegetable oil ●1 Tbsp Szechuan peppercorns ●2 Tbsp chili oil ●2 minced garlic cloves ●1 Tbsp grated ginger ●2 Tbsp soy sauce ●1 Tbsp balsamic vinegar ●1 tsp sugar ●1 Tbsp sesame paste ●½ cup shredded cucumber ●2 Tbsp chopped peanuts ●1 Tbsp chopped green onion
Directions: ●Boil noodles according to package instructions, drain and set aside ●Heat vegetable oil in a pan and fry Szechuan peppercorns until fragrant, then discard them ●In the same oil, sauté garlic and ginger, then add chili oil, soy sauce, vinegar, sugar, and

sesame paste to form a sauce ●Pour the spicy sauce over the noodles, add shredded cucumber, and toss well ●Garnish with chopped peanuts and green onion before serving

Tips: ●To balance the dish, adjust the level of spice with more or less chili oil according to taste ●Szechuan peppercorns introduce a unique tingling sensation; use sparingly if unfamiliar with their potency

Nutritional Values: Calories: 400, Fat: 22g, Carbs: 45g, Protein: 9g, Sugar: 4g

STIR-FRIED HOISIN NOODLES WITH MIXED VEGETABLES

Preparation Time: 25 min
Cooking Time: 20 min
Mode of Cooking: Stir-Frying
Servings: 4
Ingredients: ●200g flat rice noodles ●1 Tbsp vegetable oil ●1 red bell pepper, julienned ●1 cup broccoli florets ●½ cup sliced mushrooms ●¼ cup green peas ●1 sliced carrot ●1 Tbsp minced garlic ●4 Tbsp hoisin sauce ●2 Tbsp soy sauce ●1 Tbsp rice vinegar ●1 tsp chili flakes ●1 Tbsp peanut butter ●¼ cup water ●2 Tbsp chopped cilantro for garnish

Directions: ●Cook flat rice noodles according to the package directions, drain and set aside ●Heat oil in a large wok or pan over medium heat and stir-fry garlic until fragrant ●Add vegetables and cook until they are tender yet crisp ●In a small bowl, mix hoisin sauce, soy sauce, rice vinegar, chili flakes, peanut butter, and water to make a smooth sauce ●Add the sauce and cooked noodles to the wok, tossing everything together until the noodles are evenly coated and heated through ●Garnish with chopped cilantro before serving

Tips: ●To prevent rice noodles from sticking, rinse them under cold water after cooking and drain well ●Adjust the amount of chili flakes to control the spice level ●Peanut butter can be omitted for a less rich sauce

Nutritional Values: Calories: 325, Fat: 9g, Carbs: 52g, Protein: 8g, Sugar: 7g

5.2.2 SINGAPORE NOODLES

CLASSIC SINGAPORE NOODLES

Preparation Time: 15 min

Cooking Time: 10 min
Mode of Cooking: Stir-Frying
Servings: 4
Ingredients: ●8 oz. rice vermicelli noodles ●2 Tbsp curry powder ●2 Tbsp vegetable oil ●1 clove garlic, minced ●1 Tbsp fresh ginger, minced ●1 small red bell pepper, julienned ●1 small green bell pepper, julienned ●4 scallions, thinly sliced ●1 medium carrot, julienned ●6 oz. shrimp, peeled and deveined ●6 oz. boneless pork loin, thinly sliced ●2 Tbsp soy sauce ●1 Tbsp oyster sauce ●1 tsp sugar ●Salt and pepper to taste ●1 Tbsp sesame oil ●1/4 cup fresh cilantro leaves, chopped

Directions: ●Soak rice vermicelli noodles in hot water for 5 min until they are soft, then drain ●In a large wok or frying pan, heat the vegetable oil over medium-high heat ●Add garlic and ginger, stirring for about 30 seconds until fragrant ●Stir in the curry powder and cook for another 30 seconds ●Add the pork and shrimp, stir-frying until they are just cooked through, approximately 3-4 min ●Toss in the bell peppers, carrot, and scallions, stir-frying for 2-3 min until they are just tender ●Add the softened noodles to the wok along with soy sauce, oyster sauce, and sugar. Toss everything together until the noodles are evenly coated and heated through, about 2 min ●Season with salt and pepper to taste ●Drizzle with sesame oil and garnish with cilantro leaves before serving

Tips: ●Prepare ingredients before heating the wok to ensure a quick and even cooking process ●Use a high heat to stir-fry, keeping the ingredients moving to prevent burning ●For a vegetarian version, substitute tofu for the shrimp and pork, adjusting the cooking time accordingly

Nutritional Values: Calories: 350, Fat: 12g, Carbs: 45g, Protein: 18g, Sugar: 3g

SZECHUAN-STYLE STIR-FRY NOODLES

Preparation Time: 20 min
Cooking Time: 15 min
Mode of Cooking: Stir-Frying
Servings: 4
Ingredients: ●8 oz. dried thin wheat noodles ●2 Tbsp sesame oil ●1 Tbsp Szechuan peppercorns ●2 cloves garlic, minced ●1 Tbsp ginger, minced ●4 green

onions, sliced ●1 red chili, thinly sliced ●1 cup minced pork ●1/4 cup Szechuan chili paste ●2 Tbsp soy sauce ●1 Tbsp rice vinegar ●1 tsp sugar ●1 cup bean sprouts ●1/2 cup peanuts, crushed ●Salt to taste

Directions: ●Cook noodles according to package instructions then drain and set aside ●Heat sesame oil in a wok over medium heat, add Szechuan peppercorns and stir-fry for 1 min until fragrant ●Add garlic, ginger, half of the green onions, and red chili, stir-frying for 2 min ●Increase heat to high, add minced pork and stir-fry until cooked through, about 5 min ●Stir in Szechuan chili paste, soy sauce, rice vinegar, and sugar, cooking for another 2 min ●Add cooked noodles and toss until they are thoroughly coated and heated through ●Finally, stir in bean sprouts and cook for an additional 1 min ●Garnish with remaining green onions and crushed peanuts before serving

Tips: ●Prepare all ingredients ahead to ensure a seamless cooking process ●Adjust the amount of Szechuan chili paste according to your preference for spice ●Garnish with fresh cilantro for an additional layer of flavor

Nutritional Values: Calories: 520, Fat: 28g, Carbs: 54g, Protein: 20g, Sugar: 4g

BEIJING ZA JIANG MIAN

Preparation Time: 25 min
Cooking Time: 20 min
Mode of Cooking: Boiling and Stir-Frying

Servings: 4

Ingredients: ●8 oz. fresh thick wheat noodles ●2 Tbsp vegetable oil ●4 cloves garlic, minced ●1 Tbsp fresh ginger, minced ●1 lb. ground pork ●1/4 cup yellow bean sauce ●2 Tbsp hoisin sauce ●1 Tbsp dark soy sauce ●1 cup cucumber, julienned ●1 cup bean sprouts ●4 green onions, chopped ●1 tsp toasted sesame seeds

Directions: ●Boil noodles according to package instructions until al dente, drain, then rinse under cold water and set aside ●Heat oil in a large wok over medium-high heat ●Add garlic and ginger, sautéing until fragrant, about 1 min ●Add ground pork, breaking it apart with a spatula and cook until browned, about 5-7 min ●Stir in yellow bean sauce, hoisin sauce, and dark soy sauce, simmering for 10 min until thickened ●Serve the sauce over noodles, topped with cucumber, bean sprouts, green onions, and sprinkled with toasted sesame seeds

Tips: ●To achieve a balanced flavor, adjust the amount of yellow bean and hoisin sauce according to taste ●For a crunchier texture, add cucumbers and bean sprouts just before serving ●Toasted sesame seeds add a nutty flavor and appealing texture

Nutritional Values: Calories: 630, Fat: 35g, Carbs: 58g, Protein: 25g, Sugar: 7g

5.3 NOODLE SOUPS AND BROTHS

In the heart of Chinese culinary tradition lies the soul-soothing world of noodle soups and broths, a universe where each simmering pot tells a story of comfort and nourishment. These dishes, essential to any Chinese menu, are as diverse as China itself, ranging from the robust, fiery broths of Sichuan to the clear, subtle flavors of a Cantonese wonton soup.

The magic begins with the broth, the foundation upon which these dishes are built. A well-crafted broth is a testament to the patience and skill of the cook, often simmered for hours to extract the deep, nuanced flavors from bones, spices, and herbs. Into this aromatic base, noodles are introduced, absorbing the broth's essence and becoming carriers of its soul.

Floating amidst these silken strands are generous helpings of vegetables, slices of meat, or delicate dumplings, each adding their texture and flavor, complementing and completing the dish. The experience of savoring a bowl of Chinese noodle soup is both comforting and invigorating, as the warm broth nourishes the body and the vibrant ingredients delight the senses.

Preparing these soups at home invites you to slow down and appreciate the art of cooking. It's a culinary meditation, where the slow melding of flavors creates a meal that can warm the chilliest of days, soothe the weariest of souls, and bring a simple, profound joy to your table. Each sip and bite is not just sustenance but an invitation to explore the depths of Chinese culinary wisdom.

5.3.1 WONTON NOODLE SOUP

WONTON NOODLE SOUP WITH BLACK FUNGUS AND BAMBOO SHOOTS

Preparation Time: 20 min
Cooking Time: 25 min
Mode of Cooking: Stove Top
Servings: 4
Ingredients: ●For the wontons: 200g ground pork ●1 Tbsp soy sauce ●1 tsp sesame oil ●1 tsp shaoxing wine ●1 tsp ginger, minced ●1/4 cup black fungus, rehydrated and chopped ●1/4 cup bamboo shoots, finely diced ●1/4 cup green onions, chopped ●Wonton wrappers ●For the soup: 6 cups chicken broth ●2 Tbsp soy sauce ●1 Tbsp oyster sauce ●2 tsp sesame oil ●200g dried Chinese noodles ●2 bok choy, quartered ●4 shiitake mushrooms, sliced
Directions: ●Mix ground pork, soy sauce, sesame oil, shaoxing wine, ginger, black fungus, bamboo shoots, and green onions in a bowl for the wonton filling ●Place a teaspoon of filling in the center of each wonton wrapper, moisten the edges with water, fold into a triangle, and press edges to seal, then bring two opposite corners together and press again ●Bring chicken broth to a boil in a large pot and add soy sauce, oyster sauce, and sesame oil ●Add the wontons to

boiling broth and cook for 5 minutes, then add dried noodles and cook according to package instructions ●Finally, add bok choy and shiitake mushrooms, and simmer for an additional 3 minutes
Tips: ●To ensure your wontons are sealed properly, avoid overfilling and press out any trapped air as you fold ●Black fungus adds a unique texture and must be fully rehydrated before use ●For a spicier version, add a teaspoon of chili oil to the broth before serving
Nutritional Values: Calories: 350, Fat: 12g, Carbs: 44g, Protein: 18g, Sugar: 3g

GINGER SCALLION WONTON SOUP

Preparation Time: 15 min
Cooking Time: 20 min
Mode of Cooking: Stove Top
Servings: 4
Ingredients: ●For the wontons: 200g ground chicken ●2 Tbsp ginger, minced ●1/4 cup scallions, chopped ●1 Tbsp soy sauce ●1 tsp white pepper ●Wonton wrappers ●For the soup: 6 cups vegetable broth ●2 Tbsp soy sauce ●1 tsp sesame oil ●100g rice vermicelli noodles ●1 carrot, julienned ●1/2 cup snow peas, trimmed
Directions: ●Combine ground chicken, ginger, scallions, soy sauce, and white pepper in a bowl for the wonton filling ●Place a small amount of filling in the center of each wonton wrapper, wet the edges with water, fold into a packet shape, and press to seal ●In a large pot, bring vegetable broth to a boil, stir in soy sauce and sesame oil ●Carefully drop the wontons into the boiling broth, cooking for about 5 minutes until they float to the top ●Add rice vermicelli noodles, cooking per package instructions, then add carrot and snow peas, simmering for an additional 3-5 minutes until tender
Tips: ●Adding the vegetables towards the end of the cooking process retains their color and crunch

• Ginger in the filling should be finely minced for the best distribution of flavor • If rice vermicelli is not available, thin wheat noodles can be substituted, but cooking times may vary

Nutritional Values: Calories: 295, Fat: 6g, Carbs: 42g, Protein: 16g, Sugar: 4g

SPICY SICHUAN WONTON SOUP

Preparation Time: 25 min
Cooking Time: 30 min
Mode of Cooking: Stove Top
Servings: 4
Ingredients: • For the wontons: 250g ground pork • 2 Tbsp Sichuan peppercorns, crushed • 1 Tbsp chili oil • 1 tsp garlic, minced • 2 Tbsp green onions, chopped • 1 tsp soy sauce • 1/2 tsp sugar • Wonton wrappers • For the soup: 6 cups beef broth • 2 Tbsp soy sauce • 1 Tbsp chili oil • 1 tsp sugar • 200g thin wheat noodles • 2 tsp Sichuan peppercorns, for garnish

Directions: • Mix ground pork, Sichuan peppercorns, chili oil, garlic, green onions, soy sauce, and sugar in a bowl to prepare the wonton filling • Place a spoonful of filling onto each wonton wrapper, wet the edges with water, fold to form a triangle, then bring the points together and press to seal • In a large pot, bring beef broth to a simmer, incorporate soy sauce, chili oil, and sugar • Add prepared wontons to the broth and cook until they are done, roughly 5 minutes • Add thin wheat noodles into the broth, cook following package directions • Serve the soup garnished with additional Sichuan peppercorns

Tips: • Do not let the peppercorns burn when crushing to avoid bitterness • Adjust chili oil according to taste for spiciness level • Serving with a drizzle of sesame oil on top adds an aromatic richness to the soup

Nutritional Values: Calories: 375, Fat: 15g, Carbs: 45g, Protein: 20g, Sugar: 3g

5.3.2 SICHUAN SPICY HOT POT NOODLES

SICHUAN BEEF HOT POT NOODLES

Preparation Time: 30 min
Cooking Time: 1 hr
Mode of Cooking: Simmering
Servings: 4

Ingredients: • For broth: 8 cups water • 2 slices ginger, sliced • 3 cloves garlic, smashed • 1 star anise • 2 Tbsp Sichuan peppercorns • 3 Tbsp chili bean sauce • 1 Tbsp doubanjiang (fermented bean paste) • 2 tsp sugar • For the hot pot: 1/2 lb. sliced beef shank • 4 oz. dried rice noodles • 2 cups Napa cabbage, chopped • 1 cup bean sprouts • 4 green onions, chopped • 1 Tbsp sesame oil • For garnish: Cilantro, chopped • Sesame seeds

Directions: • Prepare broth by boiling water with ginger, garlic, star anise, and Sichuan peppercorns for 15 min. • Strain and return to pot, add chili bean sauce, doubanjiang, and sugar, simmer for 20 min. • Prepare rice noodles according to package instructions, set aside. • Blanch beef shank in boiling water for 30 seconds, remove and set aside. • In the simmering broth, add Napa cabbage and cook until soft, then add bean sprouts and green onions, cooking for another 2-3 min. • Just before serving, stir in sesame oil, and arrange noodles and beef in bowls. • Pour hot broth and vegetables over noodles and beef, garnish with cilantro and sesame seeds

Tips: • Use thinly sliced beef for more tender texture • Prepare noodles ahead of time and rinse under cold water to prevent sticking • Sichuan peppercorns can be adjusted for desired level of numbing spice

Nutritional Values: Calories: 310, Fat: 8g, Carbs: 34g, Protein: 22g, Sugar: 3g

SPICY SICHUAN CHICKEN NOODLE SOUP

Preparation Time: 25 min
Cooking Time: 40 min
Mode of Cooking: Boiling
Servings: 4

Ingredients: • For the soup: 8 cups chicken stock • 1 Tbsp vegetable oil • 2 Tbsp Sichuan peppercorns • 1 inch ginger, minced • 3 cloves garlic, minced • 2 Tbsp doubanjiang • 1 Tbsp soy sauce • 1 tsp sugar • For the filling: 1 lb. boneless chicken thighs, cut into strips • 4 oz. wheat noodles • 2 cups spinach leaves • For garnish: Green onions, sliced • Chili oil

Directions: • Heat oil in a large pot over medium heat, add Sichuan peppercorns, ginger, and garlic, sauté until fragrant, about 2 min. • Add doubanjiang, stir for 1 min. • Pour in chicken stock, soy sauce, and sugar, bring to a boil, then reduce to simmer for 30 min. ●Add chicken strips, cook until fully cooked, about 15 min. ●Cook noodles as per package instructions, divide among bowls. ●Just before serving, blanch spinach in boiling water for 1 min., place on top of noodles. ●Ladle hot chicken and broth over noodles and spinach, garnish with green onions and a drizzle of chili oil

Tips: ●Blanching spinach before adding to soup preserves its green color ●Use homemade chicken stock for richer flavor ●Chili oil can be adjusted according to heat preference

Nutritional Values: Calories: 295, Fat: 14g, Carbs: 18g, Protein: 24g, Sugar: 2g

MUSHROOM AND TOFU HOT POT NOODLES

Preparation Time: 20 min
Cooking Time: 30 min
Mode of Cooking: Simmering
Servings: 4
Ingredients: ●For broth: 8 cups vegetable stock ●1 Tbsp sesame oil ●2 Tbsp soy sauce ●1 Tbsp rice vinegar ●2 tsp chili flakes ●For the hot pot: 8 oz. firm tofu, cubed ●4 oz. dried udon noodles ●1 cup shiitake mushrooms, sliced ●1 red bell pepper, julienned ●1 cup baby bok choy, chopped ●For garnish: Spring onions, sliced ●Toasted sesame seeds

Directions: ●Heat sesame oil in a large pot, add vegetable stock, soy sauce, rice vinegar, and chili flakes, bring to a simmer ●Add tofu, mushrooms, bell pepper, and bok choy to the pot, simmer until vegetables are tender and tofu is heated through, about 15 min. ●Prepare udon noodles according to package instructions, rinse and divide among bowls ●Ladle the hot broth, tofu, and vegetables over the noodles ●Garnish with sliced spring onions and toasted sesame seeds

Tips: ●For an extra layer of flavor, lightly pan-fry tofu before adding to broth ●Udon noodles can be substituted with any other noodle variety for a different texture ●Adjust chili flakes based on spice tolerance

Nutritional Values: Calories: 250, Fat: 7g, Carbs: 36g, Protein: 14g, Sugar: 5g

CHAPTER 6: RICE CREATIONS

6.1 STEAMED AND STICKY RICE DISHES

Steamed and sticky rice dishes are the comforting heart of Chinese cuisine, each preparation a homage to the grain that has sustained and shaped Chinese culture for millennia. These dishes are celebrations of texture and form, where rice transforms into something magical under the influence of steam and patience.

Imagine the gentle steam rising from a bamboo steamer, unveiling a perfect mound of sticky rice, its grains clinging together in sweet unity. This is not just cooking; it's an act of preservation, embracing techniques honed over generations. In the south, sticky rice is often mixed with luscious combinations of meats, mushrooms, and sometimes sweet beans, wrapped in lotus leaves to infuse the rice with a fragrance that whispers of lush fields and rainy mornings. The versatility of rice allows it to be the star of both savory and sweet dishes. Consider the *lo mai gai*, where sticky rice becomes a savory treasure chest, filled with chicken, Chinese sausage, and scallions, each bite a complex layer of flavors and textures. Or the simple pleasure of a perfectly steamed jasmine rice, its subtle floral scent pairing flawlessly with robust stir-fries and rich sauces.

Preparing these dishes offers a moment to slow down and appreciate the art of simplicity and subtlety. It invites an exploration into the gentle, yet precise, art of timing and heat, where each grain of rice is treated with respect and care, promising a result that nourishes both body and soul.

6.1.1 CANTONESE STICKY RICE (LO MAI GAI)

CANTONESE STICKY RICE IN LOTUS LEAF (LO MAI GAI)

Preparation Time: 30 min
Cooking Time: 2 hr
Mode of Cooking: Steaming
Servings: 4
Ingredients: ●2 cups glutinous rice, soaked overnight ●4 lotus leaves, soaked in hot water until pliable ●1 Tbsp vegetable oil ●2 Chinese sausages (lap cheong), thinly sliced ●½ cup dried shrimp, soaked and drained ●1 Tbsp Shaoxing wine ●1 Tbsp soy sauce ●1 Tbsp oyster sauce ●1 tsp sesame oil ●1 tsp sugar ●¼ tsp white pepper ●½ cup diced mushrooms (preferably shiitake) ●1 Tbsp chopped scallions

Directions: ●Drain rice and set aside ●Heat oil in a pan, add Chinese sausage and dried shrimp, cook until aromatic, about 2 minutes ●Add Shaoxing wine, soy sauce, oyster sauce, sesame oil, sugar, and white pepper, stir to combine ●Add mushrooms and scallions, cook for 1 minute ●Combine sausage mixture with drained rice, mix well ●Divide rice mixture among lotus leaves, fold to enclose filling securely ●Steam for 2 hours or until rice is tender

Tips: ●Use a bamboo steamer for best results ●Ensure lotus leaves are completely soaked to become pliable and easy to fold ●If glutinous rice seems too dry after cooking, add a small amount of water or chicken stock during the steaming process for additional moisture

Nutritional Values: Calories: 350, Fat: 8g, Carbs: 58g, Protein: 15g, Sugar: 5g

PURPLE YAM AND STICKY RICE CAKE (LO MAI CHE)

Preparation Time: 45 min

Cooking Time: 1 hr

Mode of Cooking: Baking

Servings: 6

Ingredients: ●1¾ cups glutinous rice flour ●¾ cup sugar ●1 cup mashed purple yam ●1 cup coconut milk ●½ cup water ●1 tsp baking powder ●¼ tsp salt ●1 Tbsp vegetable oil for greasing ●1 Tbsp white sesame seeds for garnish

Directions: ●Preheat oven to 350°F (175°C) ●In a large bowl, combine glutinous rice flour, sugar, baking powder, and salt ●Stir in mashed purple yam, coconut milk, and water, mix until smooth ●Grease a baking dish with vegetable oil ●Pour the batter into the greased dish, smooth the top ●Sprinkle white sesame seeds on top ●Bake for 1 hour or until a toothpick inserted into the center comes out clean

Tips: ●Allow the cake to cool completely in the baking dish before slicing ●Purple yam can be substituted with taro for a different flavor profile ●Serve with a side of whipped coconut cream for added decadence

Nutritional Values: Calories: 280, Fat: 5g, Carbs: 55g, Protein: 4g, Sugar: 20g

CANTONESE STICKY RICE (LO MAI GAI)

Preparation Time: 20 min

Cooking Time: 2 hr

Mode of Cooking: Steaming

Servings: 4

Ingredients: ●2 cups glutinous rice, soaked overnight ●4 dried shiitake mushrooms, soaked and diced ●1 Chinese sausage (Lap Cheong), thinly sliced ●100g boneless chicken thigh, marinated in 1 Tbsp soy sauce & 1 tsp sesame oil ●1 Tbsp oyster sauce ●1 tsp dark soy sauce ●1 tsp sugar ●½ tsp salt ●1 Tbsp cooking wine ●4 Tbsp peanut oil ●1 scallion, finely chopped ●1 Tbsp finely grated ginger ●4 lotus leaves, soaked and cut in half

Directions: ●Rinse the soaked rice until the water runs clear, then drain ●Heat half of the peanut oil in a wok and stir-fry the chicken until just cooked, then set aside ●In the same wok, add the remaining oil, ginger, and scallions, frying until fragrant ●Add mushrooms and

sausage, cooking for 2 min. before introducing the rice, oyster sauce, dark soy sauce, sugar, salt, and cooking wine, stir well to combine and cook for another 5 min. ●Divide the rice mixture among lotus leaves, top with chicken, and wrap securely ●Steam for 1.5 hrs

Tips: ●Use a bamboo steamer for the best flavor ●Avoid overcrowding the steamer to ensure even cooking

Nutritional Values: Calories: 359, Fat: 11g, Carbs: 54g, Protein: 14g, Sugar: 2g

6.1.2 LOTUS LEAF WRAPPED RICE (LUO BO GAO)

JASMINE TEA-SCENTED LOTUS LEAF RICE

Preparation Time: 30 min.

Cooking Time: 2 hr.

Mode of Cooking: Steaming

Servings: 4

Ingredients: ●2 large lotus leaves, soaked and rinsed ●2 cups jasmine rice, washed ●1 Tbsp. sesame oil ●200g boneless chicken thighs, cut into small pieces ●4 dried shiitake mushrooms, rehydrated and chopped ●1 Tbsp. soy sauce ●1 tsp. oyster sauce ●½ tsp. white pepper ●1 Tbsp. Shaoxing wine ●100g shrimp, peeled and deveined ●½ cup green peas ●4 Tbsp. chicken stock ●1 tsp. salt ●1 Tbsp. sugar ●½ cup chopped scallions

Directions: ●Soak lotus leaves in warm water for 1 hour to soften ●Rinse jasmine rice until water runs clear, then drain ●In a skillet, heat sesame oil over medium heat and sauté chicken pieces until golden brown ●Add shiitake mushrooms, soy sauce, oyster sauce, white pepper, and Shaoxing wine to the skillet, cooking until fragrant ●Combine rice with chicken mixture, shrimp, green peas, chicken stock, salt, and sugar in a large bowl, mixing well ●Divide the mixture among the lotus leaves, folding to enclose the filling ●Steam the wrapped rice over boiling water for 1.5 hr., or until rice is tender ●Carefully unwrap the lotus leaves to serve, garnishing with chopped scallions

Tips: ●Use a steamer basket lined with parchment paper to prevent sticking ●Adjust steaming time depending on the thickness of the rice layer

Nutritional Values: Calories: 420, Fat: 9g, Carbs: 68g, Protein: 18g, Sugar: 5g

LOTUS LEAF WRAPPED SALTED EGG YOLK RICE

Preparation Time: 45 min.

Cooking Time: 2 hr.

Mode of Cooking: Steaming

Servings: 4

Ingredients: •2 large lotus leaves, soaked overnight •2 cups glutinous rice, rinsed •6 salted egg yolks •1 Tbsp. light soy sauce •2 tsp. sugar •¼ tsp. ground black pepper •1 Tbsp. sesame oil •½ cup diced Chinese sausage •¼ cup dried shrimp, soaked and drained •1 Tbsp. finely chopped ginger •½ cup diced carrots •1 Tbsp. dark soy sauce for color

Directions: •Soak glutinous rice in water for 3 hours, then drain •Marinate salted egg yolks with light soy sauce, sugar, and black pepper for 10 min. •Heat sesame oil in a pan, sauté Chinese sausage, dried shrimp, and ginger until aromatic •Add carrots and pre-soaked rice to the pan, stirring well •Stir in dark soy sauce to achieve a rich color •Divide rice mixture evenly onto the center of each lotus leaf, placing three marinated egg yolks on top of the rice in each leaf •Fold lotus leaves securely around the rice, ensuring a tight seal •Steam over high heat for 2 hr. or until rice is fully cooked •Unwrap the parcels and enjoy the fragrant rice mixed with creamy salted egg yolk

Tips: •To enhance flavor, let marinated egg yolks sit overnight in the fridge •Ensure the lotus leaves are thoroughly soaked to avoid tearing when wrapping

Nutritional Values: Calories: 465, Fat: 15g, Carbs: 70g, Protein: 13g, Sugar: 4g

SWEET COCONUT AND RED BEAN RICE IN LOTUS LEAF

Preparation Time: 35 min.

Cooking Time: 1 hr. 30 min.

Mode of Cooking: Steaming

Servings: 4

Ingredients: •2 large lotus leaves, soaked in hot water •2 cups glutinous rice, soaked for 4 hours and drained •1 cup coconut milk •¾ cup water •1 Tbsp. sugar •½ tsp. salt •1 cup red bean paste •2 Tbsp. toasted sesame seeds •1 Tbsp. vegetable oil

Directions: •Combine glutinous rice, coconut milk, water, sugar, and salt in a pot and bring to a simmer, cooking until the liquid is absorbed •Spread a thin layer of cooked rice on each lotus leaf •Place a portion of red bean paste in the center, then cover with another layer of rice, pressing down gently •Fold the lotus leaves to enclose the rice mixture •Steam the parcels over medium heat for 1 hr. •Serve hot, sprinkled with toasted sesame seeds

Tips: •Use a clean brush to evenly spread vegetable oil on the lotus leaves to prevent the rice from sticking •Wrap the parcels securely to ensure no filling escapes during steaming

Nutritional Values: Calories: 520, Fat: 10g, Carbs: 98g, Protein: 8g, Sugar: 22g

6.2 FRIED RICE VARIETIES

Fried rice, a quintessential dish in Chinese cuisine, epitomizes the ingenuity of using simple ingredients to create a symphony of flavors and textures. This dish, born from the necessity of repurposing leftover rice, has evolved into a culinary canvas that chefs and home cooks alike paint with their local flavors and personal flair.

Each region of China brings its own twist to fried rice, transforming it through local ingredients and cultural influences. In the bustling cities of the east, *Yangzhou fried rice* comes alive with vibrant peas, fresh shrimp, and the rich flavors of char siu pork, presenting a colorful palette that reflects the diversity of its origins. Further south, *pineapple fried rice* borrows sweet and tangy notes from its tropical surroundings, incorporating chunks of pineapple and the occasional curry spice for a dish that sings with bold contrasts.

The secret to perfecting fried rice lies in the balance of textures and flavors—crispy yet tender rice grains, infused with the smoky essence of the wok, mixed with crunchy vegetables and savory morsels of meat or seafood. Mastering this dish requires not just understanding the right ingredients but also the rhythm of the wok—knowing when to stir and when to let the rice sit and develop that coveted golden crust.

As you explore the various recipes, you'll learn not just how to make a dish, but how to weave the narrative of culture, tradition, and innovation into your cooking. Fried rice is more than a meal; it's a lesson in creativity and adaptation, a testament to the enduring appeal of Chinese culinary traditions.

6.2.1 YANGZHOU FRIED RICE

CLASSIC YANGZHOU FRIED RICE

Preparation Time: 15 min
Cooking Time: 10 min
Mode of Cooking: Stir-Frying
Servings: 4
Ingredients: ●2 cups jasmine rice, cooked and chilled ●2 Tbsp vegetable oil ●1 small white onion, finely chopped ●2 cloves garlic, minced ●1/2 cup peas, fresh or frozen ●1/2 cup carrots, small dice ●2 eggs, lightly beaten ●3/4 cup cooked shrimp, small ●3/4 cup char siu (Chinese BBQ pork), diced ●2 Tbsp light soy sauce ●1 Tbsp oyster sauce ●1/2 tsp white pepper ●Scallions, chopped for garnish ●Salt to taste
Directions: ●Heat oil in a large skillet or wok on medium-high heat ●Add onion and garlic, sauté until fragrant ●Stir in peas and carrots, cook until slightly tender ●Push vegetables to the side, pour in eggs, scramble until just set ●Incorporate the shrimp and char siu, stirring well ●Add the rice, breaking any clumps, ensuring even heating ●Mix in soy sauce, oyster sauce, and white pepper, stir fry until everything is well combined and hot ●Season with salt if needed, garnish with scallions before serving
Tips: ●Use day-old rice for a better texture as it prevents the fried rice from becoming mushy ●For a vegetarian option, omit shrimp and char siu, adding tofu and more vegetables instead ●Experiment with the heat level to caramelise the rice slightly for a nuttier flavor
Nutritional Values: Calories: 350, Fat: 12g, Carbs: 45g, Protein: 18g, Sugar: 3g

SHANDONG SPICED BEEF FRIED RICE

Preparation Time: 15 min
Cooking Time: 10 min
Mode of Cooking: Stir-fry
Servings: 4
Ingredients: ●2 cups of jasmine rice, precooked and chilled ●1 lb. thinly sliced beef sirloin ●2 Tbsp soy sauce ●1 Tbsp Shaoxing wine ●2 tsp cornstarch ●3 Tbsp vegetable oil ●1 tsp sichuan peppercorns, crushed ●2 cloves garlic, minced ●1 Tbsp ginger, minced ●1 medium carrot, diced ●1 red bell pepper, diced ●4 scallions, sliced ●1 tsp sesame oil ●Salt to taste
Directions: ●Combine the beef slices with soy sauce, Shaoxing wine, and cornstarch in a bowl, marinate for 10 minutes ●Heat 2 Tbsp of vegetable oil in a wok on high heat, add the beef and stir-fry until just cooked, then remove and set aside ●Add remaining 1 Tbsp vegetable oil to the wok, stir in sichuan peppercorns, garlic, and ginger until aromatic ●Add diced carrots and bell pepper, stir-fry for 2 minutes ●Incorporate the cooked beef, chilled rice, and scallions, stir well until everything is heated through and evenly mixed ●Finish with a drizzle of sesame oil, and season with salt to taste
Tips: ●Use rice that has been cooked and chilled for at least a few hours, as it fries better and won't clump together ●Feel free to substitute sirloin with other quick-cooking cuts of beef ●Garnish with additional sliced scallions for a fresh crunch
Nutritional Values: Calories: 512, Fat: 20g, Carbs: 54g, Protein: 27g, Sugar: 3g

FIVE TREASURE FRIED RICE

Preparation Time: 20 min
Cooking Time: 12 min
Mode of Cooking: Stir-fry
Servings: 4
Ingredients: ●2 cups of short-grain rice, precooked and chilled ●1/4 cup roast duck, chopped ●1/4 cup char siu pork, chopped ●1/4 cup cooked shrimp ●1/4 cup diced century egg ●1/4 cup green peas ●2 Tbsp vegetable oil ●2 Tbsp oyster sauce ●1 Tbsp soy sauce

●2 tsp sesame oil ●4 scallions, sliced ●Salt and white pepper to taste

Directions: ●Heat the vegetable oil in a large wok or frying pan over medium-high heat ●Sauté roast duck, char siu pork, shrimp, and century egg for about 3 minutes or until heated through ●Stir in the precooked and chilled rice, breaking up any clumps and ensuring the rice is evenly coated with oil ●Add oyster sauce, soy sauce, and sesame oil, mixing thoroughly ●Incorporate green peas and cook for another 2 minutes ●Season with salt and white pepper, then fold in the scallions just before serving

Tips: ●Ensure all protein components are diced to similar sizes for even cooking ●Chilling the rice overnight can help prevent it from becoming soggy when fried ●Adjust the seasoning just before serving, as the flavors will develop while cooking

Nutritional Values: Calories: 450, Fat: 16g, Carbs: 56g, Protein: 20g, Sugar: 2g

6.2.2 PINEAPPLE FRIED RICE

CLASSIC PINEAPPLE FRIED RICE

Preparation Time: 15 min
Cooking Time: 10 min
Mode of Cooking: Stir-Frying
Servings: 4
Ingredients: ●2 cups jasmine rice, cooked and chilled ●1 cup pineapple tidbits, drained ●1 large egg, lightly beaten ●2 Tbsp vegetable oil ●3 cloves garlic, minced ●1 small red bell pepper, diced ●¾ cup frozen peas and carrots, thawed ●2 Tbsp soy sauce ●1 tsp sesame oil ●½ cup roasted cashews ●2 green onions, sliced ●Salt and white pepper to taste

Directions: ●Heat 1 Tbsp vegetable oil in a wok over medium-high heat ●Add the beaten egg and scramble until fully cooked, then remove it from the wok and set aside ●Heat the remaining vegetable oil in the wok, add garlic and stir-fry until fragrant, about 30 seconds ●Add red bell pepper and stir-fry for 2 minutes ●Increase the heat to high, add the chilled rice and stir-fry for 3 minutes, breaking up any clumps ●Add the peas and carrots, pineapple tidbits, scrambled egg, roasted cashews, and green onions, tossing everything together until well combined ●Season with soy sauce, sesame oil, salt, and white pepper to taste, stir-frying for another 2 minutes or until everything is heated through

Tips: ●Use day-old rice for the best texture ●For a spicier version, add a dash of Sriracha or diced chili peppers

Nutritional Values: Calories: 350, Fat: 12g, Carbs: 53g, Protein: 8g, Sugar: 10g

THAI PINEAPPLE FRIED RICE

Preparation Time: 20 min
Cooking Time: 15 min
Mode of Cooking: Stir-Frying
Servings: 4
Ingredients: ●2 cups jasmine rice, cooked and chilled ●1 cup fresh pineapple, cubed ●2 Tbsp coconut oil ●1 large shallot, finely chopped ●2 cloves garlic, minced ●1 red chili, seeded and thinly sliced ●½ cup cashew nuts, toasted ●¼ cup raisins ●2 Tbsp fish sauce ●1 Tbsp soy sauce ●1 tsp curry powder ●¼ cup fresh cilantro, chopped ●2 green onions, sliced ●Juice of 1 lime ●1 egg, lightly beaten ●Salt to taste

Directions: ●Heat the coconut oil in a large wok or frying pan over medium-high heat ●Add shallot, garlic, and red chili, stir-frying until aromatic, about 2 minutes ●Push the ingredients to one side of the wok and add the lightly beaten egg to the other side, scramble until just set ●Mix in the chilled jasmine rice and increase heat to high, stir-frying for about 3 minutes ●Add the pineapple cubes, cashew nuts, raisins, fish sauce, soy sauce, and curry powder, mixing thoroughly until the rice is golden ●Stir in the cilantro, green onions, and lime juice right before removing from heat ●Season with salt to taste

Tips: ●Serve with lime wedges for an extra zing ●Adding a bit more curry powder will intensify the flavor for those who prefer a bolder taste

Nutritional Values: Calories: 380, Fat: 14g, Carbs: 58g, Protein: 8g, Sugar: 14g

SICHUAN PINEAPPLE FRIED RICE

Preparation Time: 20 min
Cooking Time: 12 min
Mode of Cooking: Stir-Frying
Servings: 4

Ingredients: ●2 cups jasmine rice, cooked and chilled ●1 cup pineapple chunks ●2 Tbsp peanut oil ●2 Tbsp Sichuan peppercorns, crushed ●4 spring onions, chopped ●1 red bell pepper, diced ●1 cup snap peas, trimmed ●2 Tbsp hoisin sauce ●1 Tbsp chili bean sauce (Doubanjiang) ●1 tsp dark soy sauce ●½ tsp ground ginger ●1 egg, lightly beaten ●¼ cup roasted peanuts, for garnish ●Salt to taste

Directions: ●Heat peanut oil in a wok over medium-high heat ●Add Sichuan peppercorns and stir-fry until fragrant, about 1 min ●Add the spring onions, red bell pepper, and snap peas, stir-frying for about 3 minutes ●Push the veggies to the side, add the egg to the wok, and scramble until fully cooked ●Incorporate the chilled rice, pineapple chunks, hoisin sauce, chili bean sauce, dark soy sauce, and ground ginger, mixing well and stir-frying for an additional 4-5 minutes or until everything is heated through and evenly coated with the sauce ●Garnish with roasted peanuts and add salt to taste

Tips: ●To increase the numbing sensation, add more crushed Sichuan peppercorns ●Pair with a chilled cucumber salad to balance the heat

Nutritional Values: Calories: 365, Fat: 10g, Carbs: 60g, Protein: 9g, Sugar: 12g

6.3 RICE PORRIDGE AND CONGEE RECIPES

Rice porridge and congee stand as the soothing soul of Chinese breakfasts, their gentle, creamy textures offering comfort on even the coldest mornings or on days when one seeks simple, nourishing fare. This humble dish, made primarily of rice slowly simmered until it breaks down into a soft, thick consistency, is a staple across Asia, each region tailoring it with toppings and flavors that tell tales of local tastes and traditions.

In the north, congee is often enjoyed in its purest form—subtly seasoned and sometimes accompanied by pickled vegetables or a small dish of fermented tofu. Moving south, the congee becomes a canvas for bolder flavors, such as the *Century Egg Congee*, where the potent, earthy flavors of preserved eggs meld beautifully with the mild rice base, offering a dish that challenges the palate and rewards the adventurous eater.

The preparation of congee is less about technique and more about patience; it's about allowing the rice to gradually release its starches, creating a texture that's at once creamy yet light, almost like a warm embrace. It serves not only as a meal but also as a remedy, believed to aid digestion and heal the body.

Embracing the simplicity and versatility of congee teaches the value of minimalism in cooking—a few ingredients, when given time and care, can transform into a meal that comforts the soul and delights the senses, embodying the philosophy that sometimes, less truly is more.

6.3.1 CHICKEN AND CORN CONGEE

GINGER CHICKEN CONGEE

Preparation Time: 10 min
Cooking Time: 1 hr 30 min
Mode of Cooking: Simmering
Servings: 4
Ingredients: ●1 cup jasmine rice, rinsed ●8 cups chicken broth ●2 boneless, skinless chicken thighs ●1 2-inch piece of ginger, peeled and sliced ●2 Tbsp light soy sauce ●1 Tbsp sesame oil ●1 scallion, finely chopped ●Salt to taste

Directions: ●Combine rice, chicken broth, chicken thighs, and ginger in a large pot and bring to a boil over high heat ●Reduce heat to low, cover, and simmer, stirring occasionally, until the congee is thickened and creamy, about 1 hr 30 min ●Remove chicken, shred it, and return it to the pot ●Stir in soy sauce and sesame oil, and season with salt to taste ●Serve hot, garnished with scallion

Tips: ●Use a rice cooker to simplify the cooking process ●Enhance flavor with a dash of white pepper

●Congee thickens as it cools; add broth when reheating if necessary

Nutritional Values: Calories: 350, Fat: 14g, Carbs: 40g, Protein: 18g, Sugar: 2g

MUSHROOM AND CHICKEN CONGEE

Preparation Time: 15 min
Cooking Time: 2 hr
Mode of Cooking: Simmering
Servings: 4
Ingredients: ●1 cup long grain rice, rinsed ●10 cups water ●1 lb chicken breast, cubed ●1 cup shiitake mushrooms, sliced ●1 tsp minced garlic ●1 Tbsp ginger, minced ●3 Tbsp oyster sauce ●2 Tbsp light soy sauce ●2 tsp sesame oil ●Salt and white pepper to taste ●Cilantro for garnish

Directions: ●In a large pot, combine rice and water, bringing to a boil over high heat ●Add chicken, garlic, and ginger, reducing heat to a simmer and cook for 1 hr, stirring occasionally ●Add mushrooms, oyster sauce, soy sauce, and sesame oil, continue to simmer until the congee thickens, about 1 hr more ●Season with salt and white pepper ●Serve garnished with cilantro

Tips: ●Congee can be made in advance and stored in the refrigerator for up to 3 days ●For a vegetarian version, omit chicken and use vegetable broth ●Mushroom variety can be varied based on preference

Nutritional Values: Calories: 275, Fat: 6g, Carbs: 35g, Protein: 20g, Sugar: 3g

CENTURY EGG AND LEAN PORK CONGEE

Preparation Time: 20 min
Cooking Time: 1 hr 20 min
Mode of Cooking: Simmering
Servings: 4
Ingredients: ●1 cup short grain rice, rinsed ●8 cups chicken broth ●2 century eggs, peeled and quartered ●200g lean pork, thinly sliced ●2 tsp salt ●2 Tbsp light soy sauce ●1 tsp sugar ●1 piece of ginger, julienned ●Spring onions, chopped for garnish ●Fried shallots, for garnish

Directions: ●Bring rice and chicken broth to a boil in a large pot ●Reduce heat and simmer until rice begins to break down, about 40 min ●Add pork, salt, soy sauce, sugar, and ginger, cooking until pork is tender, about 40 min more ●Gently stir in century eggs ●Serve garnished with spring onions and fried shallots

Tips: ●To avoid toughness, slice the pork as thinly as possible ●Century eggs have a strong flavor, adjust quantity to taste ●For a silkier texture, blend part of the congee before adding pork and eggs

Nutritional Values: Calories: 320, Fat: 8g, Carbs: 42g, Protein: 22g, Sugar: 2g

6.3.2 PRESERVED EGG AND PORK CONGEE

GINGER CHICKEN AND PRESERVED EGG CONGEE

Preparation Time: 15 min.
Cooking Time: 1 hr. 30 min.
Mode of Cooking: Simmering
Servings: 4
Ingredients: ●1 cup jasmine rice, rinsed ●8 cups water ●2 preserved eggs, coarsely chopped ●1 lb. boneless chicken thighs, cut into small pieces ●2 Tbsp ginger, minced ●1 Tbsp soy sauce ●1 Tbsp oyster sauce ●Salt, to taste ●White pepper, to taste ●2 green onions, finely sliced for garnish ●Cilantro leaves, for garnish ●1 tsp sesame oil

Directions: ●Combine rice and water in a large pot and bring to a boil over high heat ●Reduce heat to low, cover, and simmer for 1 hr., stirring occasionally ●Add chicken, preserved eggs, ginger, soy sauce, and oyster sauce to the pot ●Season with salt and white pepper to taste ●Cook for additional 30 min. on low heat, stirring occasionally, until chicken is fully cooked and congee has thickened to your liking ●Serve hot, garnished with green onions, cilantro, and a drizzle of sesame oil

Tips: ●Stir the congee regularly to prevent sticking and ensure even cooking ●Preserved eggs can be found at Asian markets; their unique flavor enhances this dish significantly ●Add more water for a thinner consistency if desired

Nutritional Values: Calories: 310, Fat: 8g, Carbs: 38g, Protein: 21g, Sugar: 1g

BEEF AND GINGER CONGEE

Preparation Time: 20 min.
Cooking Time: 2 hr.

Mode of Cooking: Slow Cooking

Servings: 4

Ingredients: ●1 cup long grain rice ●10 cups water ●1/2 lb. beef shank, thinly sliced ●2 Tbsp ginger, julienned ●1 Tbsp light soy sauce ●2 tsp dark soy sauce ●Salt, to taste ●White pepper, to taste ●4 Tbsp green onions, chopped ●1 preserved egg, thinly sliced ●1 Tbsp sesame oil

Directions: ●Combine rice and water in a large pot; bring to a boil, then reduce heat to low and simmer uncovered for 1 hr. 45 min., until it begins to thicken ●Add beef, ginger, light soy sauce, and dark soy sauce to the pot; season with salt and white pepper ●Continue to cook for an additional 15 min., or until beef is tender ●Serve the congee garnished with green onions, slices of preserved egg, and a drizzle of sesame oil

Tips: ●To achieve an ultra-smooth texture, stir frequently and gently break down the grains of rice during the simmering process ●Use a very low flame for cooking to avoid scorching ●This dish pairs well with pickled vegetables on the side for added flavor and texture

Nutritional Values: Calories: 275, Fat: 6g, Carbs: 40g, Protein: 15g, Sugar: 2g

MUSHROOM AND PRESERVED EGG CONGEE

Preparation Time: 10 min.

Cooking Time: 1 hr.

Mode of Cooking: Simmering

Servings: 4

Ingredients: ●1 cup short-grain rice ●8 cups chicken stock ●4 preserved eggs, quartered ●1 cup shiitake mushrooms, thinly sliced ●2 Tbsp light soy sauce ●Salt, to taste ●White pepper, to taste ●2 Tbsp chives, chopped ●2 tsp ginger, minced ●1 Tbsp sesame oil ●2 Tbsp fried shallots, for garnish

Directions: ●In a large pot, combine rice and chicken stock and bring to a simmer over medium heat ●Reduce heat to low and cook for about 50 min., stirring occasionally ●Add preserved eggs, shiitake mushrooms, light soy sauce, salt, and white pepper ●Cook for an additional 10 min. ●Serve hot, garnished with chives, ginger, a drizzle of sesame oil, and fried shallots on top

Tips: ●To enhance the umami flavor, use homemade chicken stock if possible ●The addition of fried shallots adds a delightful crunch and flavor contrast to the creamy congee ●For a vegetarian option, substitute chicken stock with vegetable broth

Nutritional Values: Calories: 200, Fat: 5g, Carbs: 32g, Protein: 8g, Sugar: 2g

CHAPTER 7: POULTRY PERFECTION

7.1 CHICKEN STIR-FRIES AND BRAISES

In the bustling kitchens of China, the sizzle of chicken hitting a hot wok is a familiar sound, heralding the start of a dish that will be both vibrant and soothing. Chicken stir-fries and braises are cornerstones of Chinese cuisine, known for their quick cooking times, colorful medley of vegetables, and deeply flavorful sauces that enliven the tender meat. The art of stir-frying chicken involves high heat and quick movement—tossing sliced or diced chicken in a glaze of soy sauce, garlic, and ginger, alongside crisp bell peppers, tender bamboo shoots, and pungent scallions. This technique not only seals in the flavors but also preserves the textures of both the meat and the vegetables, resulting in a dish that is as delightful to the palate as it is to the eye.

Braising, on the other hand, is a slower, more meditative cooking process. Here, chicken is often combined with earthier ingredients like mushrooms and star anise, and simmered in a rich sauce until it becomes fork-tender, absorbing the complex amalgamation of flavors into every bite. This method showcases the chicken's ability to act as a canvas, melding its mild flavor with the robustness of the braise.

Exploring these methods introduces not just techniques but also a philosophy of cooking—balancing speed with patience, and flavor with texture. Each dish you create is a step closer to mastering the subtle art of Chinese poultry cooking, bringing a taste of Chinese tradition to your table with each flavorful bite.

7.1.1 KUNG PAO CHICKEN

KUNG PAO CHICKEN

Preparation Time: 20 min
Cooking Time: 30 min
Mode of Cooking: Stir-Frying
Servings: 4
Ingredients: ●1 lb. boneless, skinless chicken thighs, cut into 1-inch pieces ●2 Tbsp soy sauce ●1 Tbsp Shaoxing wine ●2 tsp cornstarch ●3 Tbsp vegetable oil ●8-10 dried red chili peppers ●1 Tbsp Sichuan peppercorns ●1/2 cup unsalted roasted peanuts ●2 tsp minced garlic ●1 tsp minced ginger ●1 green bell pepper, diced ●1 red bell pepper, diced ●Sauce: 2 Tbsp soy sauce ●1 Tbsp balsamic vinegar ●1 Tbsp hoisin sauce ●1 Tbsp sugar ●2 tsp sesame oil ●1 tsp cornstarch mixed with 1 Tbsp water

Directions: ●Marinate chicken in soy sauce, Shaoxing wine, and 2 tsp cornstarch for 15 min ●Heat 2 Tbsp vegetable oil in a wok over high heat and stir-fry chicken until golden brown, remove and set aside ●In the same wok, add remaining oil, dried chilies, and Sichuan peppercorns, stir-frying until aromatic ●Add peanuts, garlic, and ginger, stir-fry for a minute ●Return chicken to the wok, add diced bell peppers ●Mix sauce ingredients and add to the wok, stirring until the sauce thickens and coats the chicken evenly

Tips: ●Use tongs to turn and evenly coat the chicken pieces in sauce to ensure even flavor coverage ●For an authentic taste, use Chinese Shaoxing wine instead of sherry or other substitutes ●Adjust the amount of dried chili peppers and Sichuan peppercorns according to your heat preference

Nutritional Values: Calories: 420, Fat: 27g, Carbs: 15g, Protein: 31g, Sugar: 5g

SICHUAN PEPPER CHICKEN WITH SNOW PEAS

Preparation Time: 20 min.

Cooking Time: 10 min.

Mode of Cooking: Stir-Frying

Servings: 4

Ingredients: ●1 lb. chicken breast, thinly sliced ●2 Tbsp soy sauce ●1 Tbsp Shaoxing wine ●2 tsp cornstarch ●3 Tbsp vegetable oil ●1 Tbsp Sichuan peppercorns ●2 cloves garlic, minced ●1 inch ginger, minced ●1 red bell pepper, julienned ●1 cup snow peas, trimmed ●1 Tbsp hoisin sauce ●1 tsp sesame oil ●Salt to taste ●Steamed rice for serving

Directions: ●Combine chicken with soy sauce, Shaoxing wine, and cornstarch, let marinate for 15 min. ●Heat 2 Tbsp vegetable oil in a wok over high heat, add Sichuan peppercorns until fragrant, then remove and discard peppercorns, keeping the oil ●Stir-fry garlic and ginger in the flavored oil for 1 min. ●Add the chicken and stir-fry until opaque ●Add red bell pepper and snow peas, stir-fry for 2 min. ●Stir in hoisin sauce and cook for another minute ●Drizzle with sesame oil and adjust salt before removing from heat ●Serve with steamed rice

Tips: ●Toast Sichuan peppercorns slightly to release their unique numbing flavor ●Use a slotted spoon to remove peppercorns to avoid biting into one unexpectedly ●Marinating chicken enhances its flavor and tenderness

Nutritional Values: Calories: 295, Fat: 12g, Carbs: 11g, Protein: 35g, Sugar: 3g

HONEY-GLAZED CHICKEN WITH LEEKS

Preparation Time: 25 min.

Cooking Time: 15 min.

Mode of Cooking: Sautéing

Servings: 4

Ingredients: ●1 lb. chicken thighs, boneless and skinless ●3 Tbsp honey ●1 Tbsp light soy sauce ●2 Tbsp dark soy sauce ●1 Tbsp rice vinegar ●1 leek, sliced into thin rounds ●4 Tbsp vegetable oil ●2 tsp sesame seeds ●Salt and pepper to taste

Directions: ●Mix honey, light and dark soy sauce, and rice vinegar in a bowl, set aside ●Season chicken thighs with salt and pepper ●Heat oil in a pan over medium heat, sauté chicken until golden on both sides ●Add leeks to the pan, cook until softened ●Pour the honey-soy mixture over chicken and leeks, let simmer until the sauce thickens and glazes the chicken ●Sprinkle with sesame seeds before serving

Tips: ●Lower the heat when adding the honey-soy mixture to prevent it from burning ●Leeks add a mild, onion-like flavor that complements the honey glaze perfectly ●Cook leeks until just tender to retain some crispness

Nutritional Values: Calories: 400, Fat: 24g, Carbs: 18g, Protein: 30g, Sugar: 12g

7.1.2 GENERAL TSO'S CHICKEN

HONEY-SESAME GENERAL TSO'S CHICKEN

Preparation Time: 20 min

Cooking Time: 25 min

Mode of Cooking: Frying

Servings: 4

Ingredients: ●For the chicken: 1 lb. chicken thighs, boneless and skinless, cut into 1-inch pieces ●½ cup cornstarch ●2 eggs, beaten ●Salt to taste ●½ cup vegetable oil for frying. For the sauce: ¼ cup chicken stock ●3 Tbsp soy sauce ●2 Tbsp honey ●1 Tbsp rice vinegar ●2 tsp sesame oil ●3 cloves garlic, minced ●1 Tbsp ginger, minced ●2 Tbsp hoisin sauce ●1 tsp chili flakes ●For garnish: 2 Tbsp sesame seeds ●2 green onions, thinly sliced

Directions: ●Season chicken pieces with salt and coat in cornstarch, then dip into beaten eggs ●Heat oil in a large skillet over medium heat and fry chicken until golden brown and cooked through, set aside on paper towel-lined plate ●In the same skillet, add garlic and ginger, sautéing until fragrant ●Stir in chicken stock, soy sauce, honey, rice vinegar, sesame oil, hoisin sauce, and chili flakes, bringing to a simmer ●Add the fried chicken back into the skillet, tossing to coat in the sauce ●Garnish with sesame seeds and green onions before serving

Tips: ●To achieve a crispier texture, let coated chicken pieces sit for 10 minutes before frying ●For a spicier dish, adjust chili flakes to taste ●Serve with steamed rice or noodles for a complete meal

Nutritional Values: Calories: 480, Fat: 22g, Carbs: 38g, Protein: 34g, Sugar: 18g

ORANGE ZEST GENERAL TSO'S CHICKEN

Preparation Time: 30 min
Cooking Time: 20 min
Mode of Cooking: Stir-frying
Servings: 4

Ingredients: ●For the chicken: 1 lb. chicken breast, cubed ●1 egg, lightly beaten ●1/4 cup + 2 Tbsp all-purpose flour ●¼ cup cornstarch ●1 tsp baking powder ●Salt and pepper to taste ●½ cup water ●Oil for frying. For the sauce: ¼ cup orange juice ●Zest of 1 orange ●¼ cup soy sauce ●2 Tbsp sugar ●1 Tbsp cornstarch mixed with 2 Tbsp water ●1 tsp sesame oil ●3 cloves garlic, minced ●1 Tbsp ginger, minced ●2 Tbsp rice vinegar ●1 Tbsp chili paste

Directions: ●In a bowl, mix flour, ¼ cup cornstarch, baking powder, salt, pepper, egg, and water to create a batter. Dip chicken pieces in batter ●Fry chicken in hot oil until golden, drain on paper towels ●For sauce: In a skillet, combine orange juice, zest, soy sauce, sugar, sesame oil, garlic, ginger, rice vinegar, and chili paste, bringing to a simmer ●Add cornstarch and water mixture, stirring until sauce thickens ●Add fried chicken to the sauce, coating evenly ●Serve immediately garnished with extra orange zest if desired

Tips: ●Use fresh orange juice and zest for a brighter flavor ●Adjust the chili paste amount for desired spice levels ●Double frying chicken pieces ensures extra crispiness

Nutritional Values: Calories: 465, Fat: 15g, Carbs: 53g, Protein: 32g, Sugar: 15g

CRISPY BAKED GENERAL TSO'S CHICKEN

Preparation Time: 15 min
Cooking Time: 45 min
Mode of Cooking: Baking
Servings: 4

Ingredients: ●For the chicken: 1 lb. chicken thighs, cubed ●1 cup panko breadcrumbs ●½ cup flour ●2 eggs, beaten ●Salt and pepper to taste. For the sauce: ½ cup chicken broth ●¼ cup soy sauce ●1 Tbsp hoisin sauce ●2 tsp sesame oil ●¼ cup honey ●3 cloves garlic, minced ●2 Tbsp ginger, grated ●1 Tbsp rice wine vinegar ●1 tsp chili flakes ●1 tsp cornstarch dissolved in 2 Tbsp water

Directions: ●Preheat oven to 425°F (220°C) ●Season chicken with salt and pepper, dredge in flour, dip in eggs, then coat in panko breadcrumbs ●Place breaded chicken on a greased baking sheet and bake for 35-40 minutes until crispy ●While chicken bakes, combine chicken broth, soy sauce, hoisin sauce, sesame oil, honey, garlic, ginger, rice wine vinegar, and chili flakes in a pan and bring to a simmer ●Add cornstarch mixture to thicken the sauce ●Toss baked chicken in the sauce, and serve immediately

Tips: ●Baking chicken instead of frying offers a healthier alternative without sacrificing crunch ●Line baking tray with parchment paper for easy cleanup ●Brushing chicken with a bit of oil before baking enhances crispiness

Nutritional Values: Calories: 395, Fat: 12g, Carbs: 45g, Protein: 28g, Sugar: 20g

7.2 DUCK AND GOOSE DELICACIES

In the rich tapestry of Chinese culinary traditions, duck and goose hold prestigious places, celebrated for their depth of flavor and the meticulous methods required to prepare them. These birds are not merely ingredients but symbols of the lavishness and artistry that Chinese cuisine can offer, particularly in dishes like Peking Duck and Cantonese Roast Goose, which are as much a feast for the eyes as they are for the palate.

The preparation of these delicacies begins long before they reach the heat of the kitchen, involving a series of intricate techniques to achieve their signature crispy skins and succulent meat. Peking Duck, for instance, is an emblematic dish of Beijing, known for its mahogany-colored, lacquered skin and tender meat, traditionally served with pancakes, sweet bean sauce, and slivers of scallion and cucumber. This dish is not just food; it's a cultural icon, requiring skills passed down through generations.

Similarly, Cantonese Roast Goose is a beloved feature in southern China, its rich flavor and juicy meat enhanced by marinating with spices and aromatics that penetrate deeply. The result is a crispy outer layer that gives way to incredibly moist and flavorful flesh, a testament to the precision and patience required in its preparation.

Embracing these recipes at home brings more than just the challenge of cooking; it offers a connection to a tradition that celebrates the bounty and beauty of nature's offerings, wrapped in the history and culture of a people who prize harmony and balance in every dish.

7.2.1 PEKING DUCK

TRADITIONAL PEKING DUCK

Preparation Time: 24 hr.
Cooking Time: 2 hrs.
Mode of Cooking: Roasting
Servings: 4
Ingredients: ●1 whole duck, approximately 5 to 6 lb ●4 Tbsp honey ●1 Tbsp white vinegar ●1 cup boiling water ●½ cup molasses ●3 Tbsp soy sauce ●2 Tbsp Shaoxing wine ●1 tsp five-spice powder ●8 cloves garlic, smashed ●4 spring onions, cut into halves ●1 cucumber, julienned ●Pancakes for serving
Directions: ●Prepare the duck by removing the innards and excess fat, rinse under cold water and pat dry ●In a bowl, mix honey, vinegar, and boiling water. Brush the duck inside and out with the mixture ●Hang the duck in a cool, ventilated place for 24 hours to dry out the skin ●Preheat the oven to 375°F (190°C) ●Mix molasses, soy sauce, Shaoxing wine, and five-spice powder. Stuff the duck with garlic and half of the spring onions ●Brush the exterior of the duck with the molasses mixture and place it on a roasting rack in the oven, breast side up ●Roast for 1 hour, then flip the duck and roast for another hour until the skin is crisp and golden ●Let the duck rest for 10 minutes, then carve and serve with the remaining spring onions, cucumber, and pancakes
Tips: ●Use a fan to help dry the skin of the duck for crispier results ●Slicing the duck can be made easier by first removing the breast and then slicing it against the grain
Nutritional Values: Calories: 620, Fat: 40g, Carbs: 30g, Protein: 45g, Sugar: 20g

HONEY GLAZED PEKING DUCK

Preparation Time: 24 hr
Cooking Time: 1 hr 30 min
Mode of Cooking: Roasting
Servings: 4
Ingredients: ●1 whole duck, approximately 5 lb ●1 Tbsp Sichuan peppercorns ●3 star anise ●1 cinnamon stick ●4 slices of ginger ●4 scallions, cut into thirds ●1 cucumber, sliced thinly ●1/4 cup honey ●2 Tbsp soy sauce ●1 Tbsp Chinese rice wine ●1 Tbsp maltose ●1/2 cup boiling water ●Mandarin pancakes for serving ●Hoisin sauce for serving
Directions: ●Begin by rinsing the duck and patting it dry with paper towels ●In a pot large enough to fit the duck, bring water to a boil and blanch the duck for about 1 minute, then remove and pat dry again ●Combine the Sichuan peppercorns, star anise, cinnamon stick, ginger slices, and scallions in a bowl, then stuff this mixture inside the duck ●Sew the duck shut or secure with skewers ●In a small bowl, mix honey, soy sauce, Chinese rice wine, and maltose with boiling water until well combined ●Brush the duck with the honey mixture, ensuring it is fully coated ●Allow the duck to dry, uncovered, in the refrigerator for 24 hours to achieve a crispy skin ●Preheat oven to 375°F (190°C) ●Place the duck on a rack in a roasting pan, breast side up, and roast for 1 hr 30 min, or until the skin is rich golden brown and crispy, basting with the honey mixture every 30 min ●Carve the duck and serve with thin cucumber slices, warm mandarin pancakes, and hoisin sauce

Tips: ●Air-drying the duck in the refrigerator is crucial for crispy skin, ensure it's fully dry before roasting ●Serve with thinly sliced cucumbers for a refreshing crunch ●Allow the duck to rest for 10 minutes before carving to ensure it retains its juices

Nutritional Values: Calories: 810, Fat: 34g, Carbs: 32g, Protein: 98g, Sugar: 24g

DUCK BREAST WITH PLUM SAUCE

Preparation Time: 2 hr

Cooking Time: 20 min

Mode of Cooking: Pan-Frying

Servings: 4

Ingredients: ●2 duck breasts, skin scored ●Salt and black pepper to taste ●1 cup red wine ●2 Tbsp sugar ●1 star anise ●1 cinnamon stick ●6 plums, pitted and quartered ●1 Tbsp balsamic vinegar

Directions: ●Season the duck breasts with salt and pepper ●Heat a skillet over medium heat, place the duck skin-side down, and cook for 8-10 min until the skin is crisped ●Flip and cook for another 5-7 min for medium-rare ●Remove the duck from the skillet and let rest ●In the same skillet, add red wine, sugar, star anise, cinnamon stick, and plums ●Cook over medium heat until the plums are soft and the sauce has reduced by half ●Stir in balsamic vinegar and remove from heat ●Slice the duck breasts thinly and serve with the plum sauce drizzled over the top

Tips: ●For extra crispy skin, press the duck breast skin-side down with a spatula during the initial cooking phase ●Let the duck rest before slicing to retain moisture ●The plum sauce can be prepared in advance and reheated for ease of service

Nutritional Values: Calories: 295, Fat: 5g, Carbs: 20g, Protein: 36g, Sugar: 15g

7.2.2 CANTONESE ROAST DUCK

TRADITIONAL CANTONESE ROAST DUCK

Preparation Time: 24 hrs

Cooking Time: 1 hr 30 mins

Mode of Cooking: Roasting

Servings: 4

Ingredients: ●1 whole duck, about 4-5 lbs ●3 Tbsp maltose ●2 Tbsp Shaoxing wine ●1 Tbsp light soy sauce ●1 Tbsp dark soy sauce ●1 tsp five-spice powder ●3 slices ginger ●4 stalks green onions, halved ●2 star anise ●1 piece of cinnamon stick ●1 tsp salt ●3 Tbsp honey mixed with 1 cup warm water for glazing

Directions: ●Dry the duck with paper towels ●mix Shaoxing wine, light and dark soy sauce, five-spice powder, and salt in a bowl ●Brush the mixture inside and outside of the duck ●Stuff the duck cavity with ginger, green onions, star anise, and cinnamon stick ●Sew the duck cavity shut and let marinate for 24 hrs in the fridge ●Preheat oven to 350°F (175°C) ●Boil a large pot of water and stir in maltose until dissolved ●Blanch the duck in the maltose solution for 1 min, then hang the duck to dry for an hour ●Brush the duck with the honey water glaze every 10 mins until it's shiny and golden, for a total of 1 hr ●Roast in the oven breast side up for 45 mins ●Flip the duck and continue roasting for another 45 mins or until fully cooked

Tips: ●Hang the duck in a cool, ventilated place to achieve the best drying results ●Use a roasting hook to ensure even cooking ●Carve the duck at the table for a traditional serving experience

Nutritional Values: Calories: 980, Fat: 64g, Carbs: 18g, Protein: 76g, Sugar: 16g

CRISPY CANTONESE DUCK

Preparation Time: 24 hr. (marination) + 30 min.

Cooking Time: 4 hr.

Mode of Cooking: Roasting and Air-Drying

Servings: 4

Ingredients: ●1 whole duck, about 5 lb. ●1 Tbsp Sichuan peppercorns ●3 star anise ●1 cinnamon stick ●4 slices of fresh ginger ●4 green onions, cut into 3-inch pieces ●¼ cup soy sauce ●2 Tbsp rice wine ●1 Tbsp honey ●1 tsp Chinese five spice ●2 Tbsp maltose ●1 cup water ●Salt to taste

Directions: ●Begin by cleaning the duck and patting it dry inside and out ●Mix salt, Sichuan peppercorns, star anise, cinnamon, and Chinese five spice in a bowl and rub the mixture inside the duck's cavity ●In a saucepan, combine soy sauce, rice wine, honey, maltose, and water and bring to a simmer, ensuring the honey and maltose dissolve ●Brush the duck with the soy mixture, then insert the ginger and green onions into the cavity ●Let the duck marinate for 24 hours in the refrigerator, uncovered, to dry the skin, occasionally rebrushing with the marinade ●Preheat the oven to 300°F (150°C) ●Place the duck on a rack in a roasting pan and roast for about 3.5 hours, basting every hour with the remaining marinade ●Increase the oven temperature to 400°F (200°C) and roast for another 30 minutes to crisp the skin ●Let the duck rest for 10 minutes before carving

Tips: ●To achieve a glossy and crispy skin, ensure the duck is thoroughly dried during the marination period ●Consider using a fan to aid in skin drying ●Carve the duck at the table to showcase the crispy skin and tender meat

Nutritional Values: Calories: 290 per serving, Fat: 14g, Carbs: 5g, Protein: 35g, Sugar: 3g

FIVE-SPICE DUCK BREAST WITH PLUM SAUCE

Preparation Time: 20 min.

Cooking Time: 25 min.

Mode of Cooking: Pan-Frying and Simmering

Servings: 2

Ingredients: ●2 duck breasts, skin on ●1 Tbsp Chinese five spice ●Salt and pepper to taste ●For the plum sauce: 4 ripe plums, pitted and chopped ●½ cup brown sugar ●¼ cup soy sauce ●2 Tbsp rice vinegar ●1 star anise ●1 cinnamon stick ●1 slice of fresh ginger

Directions: ●Score the duck breast skin in a criss-cross pattern and rub with Chinese five spice, salt, and pepper ●Heat a pan over medium heat and place the duck breasts skin side down to render the fat and crisp the skin, about 6-8 minutes ●Flip the duck breasts and cook for another 6-7 minutes for medium rare ●For the plum sauce, combine plums, brown sugar, soy sauce, rice vinegar, star anise, cinnamon, and ginger in a saucepan over medium heat ●Simmer until plums are soft and the sauce has thickened, about 20 minutes, then strain ●Slice the duck breasts and serve with the warm plum sauce

Tips: ●Let the duck rest for 5 minutes before slicing to retain juices ●Cook the plum sauce while the duck rests for efficient time management ●Adjust the sweetness of the sauce to preference by adding more or less sugar

Nutritional Values: Calories: 420 per serving, Fat: 15g, Carbs: 40g, Protein: 30g, Sugar: 35g

7.3 FRAGRANT CHICKEN SOUPS AND BROTHS

The gentle simmer of a pot on the stove, filled with the makings of chicken soup, is a universal sign of home, comfort, and healing. In Chinese cuisine, chicken soups and broths are revered not just for their soothing qualities but also for their health benefits, imbued with ingredients that are chosen as much for their flavor as for their medicinal properties. Chinese chicken soups vary widely across regions but share a common foundation: a clear, deeply flavored broth that results from hours of slow cooking, allowing the essence of the chicken and aromatics to meld harmoniously. These broths are often enhanced with ginseng, goji berries, and ginger, ingredients known for their health-giving properties. One of the most beloved soups is the Chinese Chicken and Sweet Corn Soup, a dish that combines the subtle sweetness of corn with the richness of chicken in a broth that is both light and satisfying. This soup, often thickened with a touch of cornstarch and enriched with egg ribbons, represents comfort in a bowl, perfect for both chilly winter nights and as a gentle remedy during flu season.

Preparing these soups invites a meditative approach to cooking, one that values patience and the nurturing aspects of food. Each ingredient is added at just the right moment to preserve its texture and enhance the overall harmony of the dish, culminating in a broth that nourishes the body, soothes the soul, and comforts the heart.

7.3.1 CHINESE CHICKEN AND SWEET CORN SOUP

GINGKO NUT AND CHICKEN SOUP

Preparation Time: 20 min

Cooking Time: 1 hr 30 min

Mode of Cooking: Stove Top

Servings: 4

Ingredients: ●4 cups water ●1 lb chicken thighs, bone-in and skin-on ●1 cup gingko nuts, peeled and blanched ●2 slices ginger ●2 scallions, chopped into 2-inch pieces ●Salt to taste ●¼ cup Chinese cooking wine ●2 Tbsp goji berries

Directions: ●Bring water to a boil in a large pot ●Add chicken thighs, ginger, and scallions, reducing heat to a simmer and cook for 30 min ●Skim off any foam that forms on the surface ●Add gingko nuts and continue to simmer for another hour ●Season with salt and Chinese cooking wine, then add goji berries in the last 5 min of cooking

Tips: ●To peel gingko nuts, lightly crack the shells and blanch in boiling water for easy peeling ●Goji berries add a hint of sweetness and a wealth of health benefits, including improving eye health●Serve hot as a nourishing start to a meal

Nutritional Values: Calories: 285, Fat: 15g, Carbs: 12g, Protein: 22g, Sugar: 5g

SILKIE CHICKEN SOUP WITH CHINESE HERBS

Preparation Time: 25 min

Cooking Time: 2 hr

Mode of Cooking: Stove Top

Servings: 6

Ingredients: ●1 Silkie chicken (about 1.5 lb), cleaned and cut into pieces ●8 cups water ●1/4 cup Shaoxing wine ●1/2 cup dried wolfberries ●1/4 cup dried red dates, pitted ●1/4 cup dried angelica root ●6 slices astragalus root ●2 slices ginger ●Salt, to taste

Directions: ●Rinse the Silkie chicken under cold water and place it in a large pot with the 8 cups water over high heat ●Bring to a boil, then add Shaoxing wine, wolfberries, red dates, angelica root, astragalus root, and ginger ●Reduce heat to low and cover, simmering for 2 hr ●Season with salt to taste before serving

Tips: ●Silkie chicken, known for its black skin and rich, gamey flavor, elevates this soup ●Astragalus root and angelica root are known for their health-boosting properties, particularly for bolstering the immune system ●To enhance flavor, lightly brown the Silkie chicken pieces before adding water

Nutritional Values: Calories: 210, Fat: 6g, Carbs: 9g, Protein: 29g, Sugar: 4g

CHICKEN SOUP WITH LOTUS SEEDS AND RED DATES

Preparation Time: 15 min

Cooking Time: 2 hr

Mode of Cooking: Stove Top

Servings: 5

Ingredients: ●1 lb chicken pieces, bone-in ●5 cups water ●1 cup lotus seeds, soaked overnight and drained ●1/2 cup red dates, pitted ●2 slices ginger ●1 Tbsp Shaoxing wine ●Salt to taste

Directions: ●Place chicken pieces in a large pot with water and bring to a boil ●Add soaked lotus seeds, red dates, ginger, and Shaoxing wine ●Reduce heat to a low simmer and cover the pot ●Cook for about 2 hr, until the chicken is tender and the lotus seeds are soft ●Season with salt to taste before serving

Tips: ●Soaking lotus seeds overnight will soften them, making it easier to cook ●Adding Shaoxing wine complements the sweetness of the red dates and the nuttiness of the lotus seeds ●This soup is known for its soothing qualities and is perfect for recuperation

Nutritional Values: Calories: 260, Fat: 8g, Carbs: 18g, Protein: 30g, Sugar: 5g

7.3.2 GINSENG CHICKEN SOUP

GINSENG CHICKEN SOUP WITH GOJI BERRIES

Preparation Time: 20 min.

Cooking Time: 2 hr.

Mode of Cooking: Simmering

Servings: 4

Ingredients: ●1 whole chicken, about 3 lb., cleaned and gutted ●4 slices of fresh ginseng root ●¼ C. goji berries ●6 cups chicken broth ●1 large piece of ginger, sliced ●3 green onions, chopped ●Salt to taste ●A few jujubes (Chinese dates) for sweetness

Directions: ●Begin by rinsing the chicken under cold water and ensure it is thoroughly cleaned ●In a large pot, bring the chicken broth to a boil, then add the chicken, ginseng slices, and ginger ●Reduce the heat to a gentle simmer and cover the pot, allowing it to cook for 1.5 hr. ●Add the goji berries, jujubes, and half of the green onions, cooking for an additional 30 min. ●Season with salt to taste and garnish with the remaining green onions before serving

Tips: ●Try adding a small piece of star anise for a deeper flavor complexity, but remember to remove it before serving ●Keep the simmer gentle to ensure the chicken remains tender and does not fall apart ●Serve hot, ideally in deep bowls to enjoy the broth

Nutritional Values: Calories: 210, Fat: 5g, Carbs: 8g, Protein: 30g, Sugar: 4g

BLACK CHICKEN GINSENG SOUP

Preparation Time: 15 min.

Cooking Time: 3 hr.

Mode of Cooking: Slow Cooking

Servings: 6

Ingredients: ●1 Silkie chicken, cleaned and cut into large chunks ●5 slices of fresh ginseng root ●½ C. Chinese yam (Dioscorea), sliced ●10 red dates ●5 shiitake mushrooms, soaked and sliced ●1 knob of ginger, sliced ●8 cups of water ●Salt to taste

Directions: ●Place all ingredients except for salt into a large soup pot or a slow cooker ●Cover with water and cook on a low heat setting for about 3 hr., until the chicken meat is tender and falling off the bone ●Season with salt according to your taste ●Serve the soup in bowls, making sure to include a balanced mix of chicken, mushrooms, and yam in each serving

Tips: ●Use a strainer to remove any impurities that rise to the top during the first hour of cooking for a clearer broth ●The soup can be refrigerated overnight to enhance its flavors, making it a perfect prepare-ahead dish ●Due to the potent nature of ginseng, it's wise to consume this soup in moderation

Nutritional Values: Calories: 175, Fat: 4g, Carbs: 10g, Protein: 25g, Sugar: 5g

GINSENG AND LOTUS SEED CHICKEN SOUP

Preparation Time: 10 min.

Cooking Time: 2.5 hr.

Mode of Cooking: Boiling

Servings: 5

Ingredients: ●1 whole chicken, cut into pieces ●6 slices of ginseng root ●½ C. lotus seeds, soaked overnight and peeled ●6 cups of water ●2 slices of ginger ●Salt to taste

Directions: ●Start by placing the chicken pieces in a large soup pot and covering them with water ●Bring to a boil and skim off any foam that forms on the surface ●Add the ginseng root, lotus seeds, and ginger to the pot ●Reduce the heat to low, cover, and simmer for 2 hr., until the chicken is tender and the lotus seeds are soft ●Season with salt to your liking and serve warm

Tips: ●Adding a teaspoon of Chinese rice wine can elevate the soup's aroma ●Lotus seeds can be found in Asian grocery stores, ensure they are soaked and peeled for a softer texture in the soup ●For a richer broth, the chicken can be browned in a pan before adding to the pot

Nutritional Values: Calories: 220, Fat: 6g, Carbs: 12g, Protein: 32g, Sugar: 3g

CHAPTER 8: PORK PLEASURES

8.1 SWEET AND SOUR PORK

Sweet and Sour Pork, a dish that dances on the taste buds with its vibrant flavors, is a beloved classic in Chinese cuisine and a testament to the culinary philosophy of balancing opposites. This dish combines the tender, savory goodness of pork with a glossy sauce that tantalizes with its bright sweetness and sharp tanginess, creating a harmony that is both exciting and comforting.

Originating from the provinces where contrasts in flavors are celebrated, Sweet and Sour Pork has evolved into a dish that symbolizes the joy of eating and the art of cooking. The pork, often marinated and then deep-fried to golden perfection, becomes the perfect canvas for the sauce—a blend of pineapple juice, vinegar, and sugar, speckled with colorful bell peppers and pineapple chunks. These ingredients not only add layers of flavor but also create a visual feast, making the dish as delightful to look at as it is to eat.

Cooking Sweet and Sour Pork at home is an opportunity to delve into the subtleties of flavor balancing. It teaches the importance of precision in culinary timing—the crispness of the pork coating, the tenderness of the meat, and the viscosity of the sauce must all align perfectly to achieve the signature allure of this iconic dish.

As you prepare and savor your creation, you're not just feeding your household; you're engaging in a culinary tradition that delights in the playful and profound symphony of flavors—a celebration of what Chinese cuisine holds dear.

8.1.1 CLASSIC SWEET AND SOUR PORK

HONEY GLAZED SWEET AND SOUR PORK

Preparation Time: 20 min
Cooking Time: 25 min
Mode of Cooking: Stir-Frying
Servings: 4
Ingredients: ●1 lb. pork tenderloin, cubed ●1 tsp salt ●½ tsp white pepper ●2 Tbsp cornstarch ●1 Tbsp vegetable oil ●1 red bell pepper, cubed ●1 green bell pepper, cubed ●1 yellow bell pepper, cubed ●1 onion, cubed ●1/3 cup rice vinegar ●¼ cup tomato ketchup ●3 Tbsp honey ●2 Tbsp soy sauce ●1 tsp ginger, minced ●2 garlic cloves, minced ●1 tsp sesame oil ●¼ cup water ●2 Tbsp green onions, chopped for garnish
Directions: ●Season pork cubes with salt and white pepper, then coat evenly with cornstarch ●Heat vegetable oil in a wok or large skillet over medium-high heat before adding the pork cubes ●Stir-fry until they are golden brown and set aside ●In the same pan, add a little more oil if needed and stir-fry bell peppers and onion until just tender ●For the sauce, whisk together rice vinegar, ketchup, honey, soy sauce, ginger, garlic, and water in a bowl ●Pour sauce over the vegetables in the pan, add the cooked pork back in, and mix well until the pork is glazed and the sauce thickens slightly ●Drizzle with sesame oil and garnish with green onions before serving
Tips: ●Serve over steamed rice for a complete meal ●For extra crispiness, deep-fry coated pork before tossing in the sauce ●Garnish with sesame seeds for added texture

Nutritional Values: Calories: 320, Fat: 12g, Carbs: 35g, Protein: 22g, Sugar: 22g

CLASSIC SWEET AND SOUR PORK

Preparation Time: 20 min
Cooking Time: 25 min
Mode of Cooking: Stir-Fry
Servings: 4

Ingredients: ●For the pork: 500g pork loin, cut into bite-sized pieces ●1 tsp salt ●½ tsp white pepper ●2 Tbsp soy sauce ●1 egg, beaten ●1 cup cornstarch ●Oil for frying. For the sauce: ⅓ cup white vinegar ●¼ cup sugar ●2 Tbsp ketchup ●2 Tbsp soy sauce ●½ cup water ●1 tsp cornstarch dissolved in 2 Tbsp water. For the vegetables: 1 green bell pepper, diced ●1 red bell pepper, diced ●1 yellow bell pepper, diced ●1 onion, diced ●1 carrot, julienned ●Pineapple chunks, optional

Directions: ●Marinade pork with salt, white pepper, and soy sauce for 15 min ●Coat marinated pork evenly with beaten egg, then dredge in cornstarch ●Deep fry pork in hot oil until golden brown, remove and drain on paper towels ●Mix vinegar, sugar, ketchup, soy sauce, and water in a saucepan, bring to a boil. Add dissolved cornstarch, stir until sauce thickens ●Stir-fry vegetables until tender-crisp, return pork to the wok, add pineapple if using, pour sauce over, and mix well

Tips: ●Use a thermometer to ensure oil is at 350°F (177°C) for frying, ensuring crispy pork ●For a healthier version, air-fry pork pieces at 400°F (204°C) for 20 min ●Garnish with sesame seeds and sliced green onions for extra flavor and presentation

Nutritional Values: Calories: 585, Fat: 22g, Carbs: 68g, Protein: 25g, Sugar: 18g

SZECHUAN SWEET AND SOUR PORK

Preparation Time: 15 min
Cooking Time: 20 min
Mode of Cooking: Stir-Fry
Servings: 4

Ingredients: ●For the pork: 400g pork tenderloin, thinly sliced ●1 Tbsp Szechuan peppercorns, crushed ●1 Tbsp dark soy sauce ●2 tsp Chinese black vinegar ●1 egg white ●1 cup sweet potato flour ●Oil for frying. For the sauce: 2 Tbsp Chinese black vinegar ●2 Tbsp brown sugar ●2 Tbsp dark soy sauce ●1 Tbsp chili paste ●⅓ cup water ●1 tsp sesame oil. For the

vegetables: 2 cloves garlic, minced ●1 Tbsp ginger, minced ●1 red bell pepper, cut into pieces ●1 green bell pepper, cut into pieces ●Spring onions for garnishing

Directions: ●Combine pork with Szechuan peppercorns, soy sauce, Chinese black vinegar, and egg white, marinate for 10 min ●Coat pork slices with sweet potato flour, deep fry until crispy, drain on paper towels ●For sauce, combine vinegar, sugar, soy sauce, chili paste, water, and sesame oil in a pan and bring to a simmer ●Stir-fry garlic, ginger, and bell peppers until fragrant, add pork and sauce, toss well ●Garnish with spring onions

Tips: ●Adding Szechuan peppercorns to the marinade gives a distinctive numbing sensation typical of Szechuan cuisine ●Sweet potato flour creates a unique, crispy texture ●Serve with steamed rice to balance the bold flavors

Nutritional Values: Calories: 495, Fat: 18g, Carbs: 55g, Protein: 30g, Sugar: 16g

8.1.2 HONG SHAO ROU (RED-BRAISED PORK BELLY)

SZECHUAN-STYLE CRISPY PORK BELLY

Preparation Time: 15 min
Cooking Time: 2 hr
Mode of Cooking: Roasting
Servings: 4

Ingredients: ●2 lb. pork belly, skin scored ●2 Tbsp Chinese five-spice powder ●1 Tbsp Szechuan peppercorns, crushed ●1 Tbsp sea salt ●2 Tbsp light soy sauce ●2 Tbsp rice wine ●1 Tbsp honey ●4 garlic cloves, minced ●2 inch piece ginger, grated ●½ cup chicken broth

Directions: ●Preheat your oven to 375°F (190°C) ●Mix the Chinese five-spice powder, Szechuan peppercorns, and sea salt together and rub all over the pork belly, ensuring to get into the scored skin ●In a separate bowl, combine soy sauce, rice wine, honey, minced garlic, and grated ginger to create a marinade ●Place the pork belly in a roasting pan, pour over the marinade, and let it sit for 10 min ●Pour chicken broth into the bottom of the pan, ensuring not to wash off the spices from the meat ●Cover with foil and roast for 1 hr ●Remove foil, increase the oven temperature to 425°F (220°C), and roast for another 30 min or until the skin is crispy ●Let rest before slicing

Tips: ●Use a sharp knife to score the pork belly skin for maximum crispiness ●Baste the pork belly with the pan juices halfway through cooking for extra flavor

Nutritional Values: Calories: 980, Fat: 94g, Carbs: 2g, Protein: 32g, Sugar: 1g

HONEY GLAZED CHAR SIU (CHINESE BBQ PORK)

Preparation Time: 20 min
Cooking Time: 1 hr
Mode of Cooking: Grilling
Servings: 4
Ingredients: ●2 lb. pork shoulder, sliced into strips ●¼ cup honey ●¼ cup hoisin sauce ●2 Tbsp dark soy sauce ●2 Tbsp light soy sauce ●1 Tbsp Chinese rice wine (Shaoxing) ●1 Tbsp oyster sauce ●1 tsp Chinese five-spice powder ●3 Tbsp brown sugar ●5 garlic cloves, minced ●1 Tbsp fresh ginger, grated

Directions: ●Marinate the pork shoulder strips in a mixture of honey, hoisin sauce, dark and light soy sauce, Shaoxing wine, oyster sauce, Chinese five-spice, brown sugar, minced garlic, and grated ginger for at least 1 hr or overnight for best results ●Preheat your grill to medium-high heat (around 400°F or 204°C) ●Place pork strips on the grill, reserving the marinade for basting ●Grill for 10 min on each side, basting frequently with the reserved marinade, until cooked through and caramelized ●Slice and serve hot

Tips: ●Marinate the pork overnight for deeper flavor ●Slice the pork thinly against the grain to ensure tenderness ●Use a grill basket if you're worried about the pork sticking to the grill grates

Nutritional Values: Calories: 475, Fat: 13g, Carbs: 36g, Protein: 50g, Sugar: 28g

BLACK BEAN GARLIC PORK

Preparation Time: 15 min
Cooking Time: 25 min
Mode of Cooking: Stir-frying
Servings: 4
Ingredients: ●1 lb. pork belly, thinly sliced ●3 Tbsp fermented black beans, rinsed and mashed ●2 Tbsp vegetable oil ●1 Tbsp garlic, minced ●1 red bell pepper, sliced ●1 green bell pepper, sliced ●2 Tbsp soy sauce ●1 Tbsp Shaoxing wine ●1 tsp sugar ●¼ cup water ●2 Tbsp green onions, chopped for garnish

Directions: ●Heat vegetable oil in a large wok over high heat ●Add minced garlic and mashed black beans, stir-fry for 1 min ●Add pork belly slices, and stir-fry until they begin to brown, about 5 min ●Add red and green bell peppers, stir-fry for another 3 min ●Mix in soy sauce, Shaoxing wine, sugar, and water, and bring to a simmer ●Reduce heat to medium, cover, and let cook for 15 min, stirring occasionally ●Garnish with green onions before serving

Tips: ●Make sure to slice the pork belly thinly for quick cooking ●Fermented black beans can be found in Asian markets or online ●Add a splash of water if the sauce thickens too much during cooking

Nutritional Values: Calories: 790, Fat: 70g, Carbs: 6g, Protein: 38g, Sugar: 3g

8.2 PORK DUMPLINGS AND POTSTICKERS

In the realm of Chinese culinary delights, pork dumplings and potstickers hold a special place, embodying the joy of gathering and the artistry of dumpling making. These delectable morsels, whether boiled, steamed, or pan-fried, are not just a treat for the palate but a cultural ritual that brings people together, particularly during festive occasions like the Lunar New Year.

Pork dumplings, or *shui jiao*, are tender parcels filled with a juicy mixture of ground pork, ginger, and scallions, encased in a thin dough that is pleated with precision. The skill in crafting these dumplings lies in balancing the filling and the wrapper to achieve a delightful contrast in textures—soft yet resilient, flavorful yet not overpowering.

Potstickers, or *guo tie*, present a different experience. These dumplings are first pan-fried to create a crispy bottom, then steamed to ensure the filling is succulent and the top of the wrapper tender. The dual cooking method gives potstickers their characteristic texture and name, as they "stick to the pot" before they are finished with a flourish of steam.

Making these dumplings at home is a journey into the heart of Chinese culinary traditions, where technique and patience are as important as the ingredients. Each fold of the dumpling is a testament to the care and thought put into its creation, making the final dish not only a pleasure to eat but also a celebration of craftsmanship and familial bonds. As you savor each bite, consider the history and hands that shaped this culinary treasure.

8.2.1 SHUI JIAO (BOILED PORK DUMPLINGS)

TRADITIONAL SHUI JIAO (BOILED PORK DUMPLINGS)

Preparation Time: 30 min
Cooking Time: 10 min
Mode of Cooking: Boiling
Servings: 4
Ingredients: ●For the dough: 2 cups all-purpose flour ●¾ cup boiling water ●For the filling: 1 lb ground pork ●2 Tbsp soy sauce ●1 Tbsp sesame oil ●1 tsp white pepper ●4 green onions, finely chopped ●1 Tbsp ginger, minced ●2 cloves garlic, minced ●For serving: Black vinegar ●Soy sauce ●Chili oil
Directions: ●Start by making the dough: gradually pour the boiling water into the flour, mixing continuously until a dough forms ●Knead the dough on a floured surface until smooth, then cover with a damp cloth and let it rest for 20 min. ●For the filling, combine ground pork, soy sauce, sesame oil, white pepper, green onions, ginger, and garlic in a bowl, mixing thoroughly ●Roll the dough into a long snake, about 1-inch in diameter, and cut into pieces about 1-inch thick too. Flatten each piece into a circle with the palm of your hand and then roll out into a round wrapper with a rolling pin, making the edges thinner than the center ●Place a spoonful of filling in the center of each wrapper, fold in half, and pinch the edges to seal, making sure there are no air pockets ●Bring a large pot of water to a boil and cook the dumplings in batches, ensuring they don't stick together, for about 10 min, or until they float to the surface and the filling is cooked through ●Serve hot with black vinegar, soy sauce, and chili oil for dipping
Tips: ●Dough can be made in advance and kept under a damp cloth to prevent drying out ●After sealing, dumplings can be frozen on a tray before transferring to a freezer bag for later use ●Experiment with the thickness of the dough and the amount of filling to find your perfect dumpling
Nutritional Values: Calories: 350, Fat: 15g, Carbs: 35g, Protein: 20g, Sugar: 2g

SICHUAN STYLE SHUI JIAO

Preparation Time: 45 min
Cooking Time: 30 min
Mode of Cooking: Boiling
Servings: 4
Ingredients: ●For the Dough: 2 cups all-purpose flour ●3/4 cup boiling water ●For the Filling: 1 lb ground pork ●2 Tbsp Sichuan peppercorns, toasted and ground ●1 Tbsp soy sauce ●2 tsp sesame oil ●1/4 cup green onions, finely chopped ●2 Tbsp fresh ginger, minced ●2 cloves garlic, minced ●1 tsp salt ●For Dipping Sauce: 1/4 cup soy sauce ●2 Tbsp rice vinegar ●1 tsp sesame oil ●1 tsp chili oil ●1 tsp sugar ●1 Tbsp fresh cilantro, chopped
Directions: ●Mix flour with boiling water until a dough forms, then knead until smooth. Allow to rest covered for 30 min ●Mix together ground pork, Sichuan peppercorns, soy sauce, sesame oil, green onions, ginger, garlic, and salt for filling ●Roll out dough and cut into circles. Place a spoonful of filling in the center of each dough circle, fold, and seal edges ●Bring a large pot of water to a boil. Cook dumplings in batches until they float and are thoroughly cooked, about 8 min per batch ●Mix dipping sauce ingredients in a bowl ●Serve dumplings hot with dipping sauce on the side
Tips: ●Avoid overfilling dumplings to prevent them from bursting during cooking ●To seal dumplings, moisten edges of the dough with water to ensure they

stick together ●Sichuan peppercorns can be adjusted according to spice tolerance

Nutritional Values: Calories: 510, Fat: 20g, Carbs: 56g, Protein: 25g, Sugar: 2g

GINGER PORK SHUI JIAO

Preparation Time: 40 min
Cooking Time: 25 min
Mode of Cooking: Boiling
Servings: 4

Ingredients: ●For the Dough: 2.5 cups all-purpose flour ●1 cup hot water ●For the Filling: 1 lb ground pork ●3 Tbsp fresh ginger, finely grated ●1 Tbsp Shaoxing wine ●1 Tbsp soy sauce ●1 tsp sesame oil ●3 Tbsp chives, chopped ●2 tsp cornstarch ●Salt and white pepper to taste ●For Dipping Sauce: 1/4 cup soy sauce ●2 Tbsp black vinegar ●1 Tbsp ginger, julienned ●1 garlic clove, minced ●A pinch of sugar

Directions: ●Mix flour with hot water until dough forms; knead until smooth, then let rest for 30 min covered ●Combine ground pork, ginger, Shaoxing wine, soy sauce, sesame oil, chives, cornstarch, salt, and white pepper for filling ●Roll dough into thin sheet and cut into circles. Spoon filling into center, fold and press to seal ●Boil dumplings until they rise to the surface and are cooked through, approximately 7 min ●For dipping sauce, combine all ingredients and mix well ●Serve dumplings immediately with dipping sauce

Tips: ●Use a bamboo steamer to keep cooked dumplings warm while preparing the rest ●Fresh ginger in the dipping sauce enhances the dumplings' flavor ●Adjust the amount of soy sauce in the dipping sauce to control the saltiness according to preference

Nutritional Values: Calories: 495, Fat: 18g, Carbs: 62g, Protein: 23g, Sugar: 1g

8.2.2 GUO TIE (PAN-FRIED POTSTICKERS)

TRADITIONAL PORK GUO TIE (PAN-FRIED POTSTICKERS)

Preparation Time: 30 min
Cooking Time: 10 min
Mode of Cooking: Pan-Frying
Servings: 4

Ingredients: ●For the filling: 500g ground pork ●2 tsp ginger, minced ●2 Tbsp soy sauce ●1 Tbsp sesame oil ●1 cup napa cabbage, finely chopped and salted ●2 green onions, finely sliced ●½ tsp white pepper ●For the dough: 2 cups all-purpose flour ●¾ cup boiling water ●For cooking: 2 Tbsp vegetable oil ●½ cup water

Directions: ●Start by making the dough: pour the boiling water over the flour, mixing with a spoon until a dough forms ●Knead the dough on a floured surface until smooth, then let it rest covered for 20 min ●Mix together all the filling ingredients in a bowl until well combined ●Divide the rested dough into small balls and roll each into a thin circle ●Place a spoonful of filling in the center of each dough circle, fold and pinch the edges to seal ●Heat oil in a pan over medium heat, place potstickers in the pan, flat side down, and cook until the bottom is golden brown ●Add water to the pan and cover immediately, steam until the water has evaporated and the potstickers are cooked through

Tips: ●Use a damp towel to cover the dough while you work to prevent drying ●For an extra crispy bottom, let the potstickers fry for an additional minute after the water has evaporated

Nutritional Values: Calories: 350, Fat: 18g, Carbs: 28g, Protein: 16g, Sugar: 1g

SICHUAN SPICY PORK GUO TIE

Preparation Time: 35 min
Cooking Time: 12 min
Mode of Cooking: Pan-Frying
Servings: 4

Ingredients: ●For the filling: 500g ground pork ●1 Tbsp Sichuan peppercorns, crushed ●3 Tbsp chives, finely chopped ●2 tsp ginger, minced ●2 Tbsp soy sauce ●1 Tbsp chili oil ●1 tsp sichuan vinegar ●½ tsp salt ●For the dough: 2 cups all-purpose flour ●¾ cup hot water ●For cooking: 2 Tbsp vegetable oil ●½ cup water

Directions: ●Prepare the dough by mixing the hot water into the flour gradually until a soft dough forms, knead until elastic, cover, and rest it for about 20 min ●Combine all filling ingredients thoroughly in a bowl ●Divide the dough into small pieces, roll each into a round wrapper, and place a portion of the filling in the center •Fold and seal each dumpling, ensuring no filling escapes •Heat oil in a skillet over medium heat, add the Guo Tie, frying until the bottoms turn golden •Pour in water and cover immediately, let steam until the water is completely evaporated •Uncover and cook for an extra minute to crisp up the bottom

Tips: •Do not overcrowd the pan to ensure even cooking and browning •Adjust the amount of chili oil based on your spice preference •To make sure Guo Tie doesn't stick to the pan, use a non-stick pan or ensure the oil is hot before adding the dumplings

Nutritional Values: Calories: 370, Fat: 20g, Carbs: 30g, Protein: 17g, Sugar: 2g

---

GREEN ONION AND PORK GUO TIE

Preparation Time: 40 min
Cooking Time: 10 min
Mode of Cooking: Pan-Frying
Servings: 4
Ingredients: •For the filling: 400g ground pork •1 cup green onions, finely chopped •2 Tbsp soy sauce •1 Tbsp oyster sauce •1 tsp sugar •2 tsp sesame oil •¼ cup bamboo shoots, finely chopped •¼ tsp black pepper •For the dough: 2 cups all-purpose flour •¾ cup warm water •For cooking: 2 Tbsp vegetable oil •½ cup water

Directions: •Make the dough by mixing flour and warm water until a dough forms, then knead until smooth and let it rest covered for 20 min •Combine all the ingredients for the filling in a large bowl until evenly mixed •Split the dough into small, equal pieces, roll them into circles, fill with the mixture, and securely seal the edges •In a heated pan with oil, fry the sealed Guo Tie until they are golden on the bottom •Add water and cover with a lid, allow to steam until the Guo Tie is thoroughly cooked and water has evaporated •If desired, fry for an additional minute for extra crispness

Tips: •Roll the dough as thinly as possible for a tender bite •Mixing a little oil into the dough can make it more pliable and easier to work with •To enhance flavor, let the filling marinate for 10-15 min before assembling the Guo Tie

Nutritional Values: Calories: 315, Fat: 15g, Carbs: 25g, Protein: 18g, Sugar: 1g

8.3 SPICY PORK STIR-FRIES AND STEWS

The vibrant heat of Sichuan and Hunan cuisines comes alive in spicy pork stir-fries and stews, dishes that ignite the senses and warm the heart with their fiery spices and rich flavors. These recipes are not merely about the thrill of heat but also the depth and complexity that spices bring to the tender, savory pork.

Spicy pork stir-fries, like the famous *Twice-Cooked Pork*, balance the heat of chili peppers with the earthy sweetness of fermented black beans and the crisp texture of vegetables like bell peppers and leeks. This dish is a harmonious medley of flavors and textures, showcasing the pork's ability to absorb and enhance the bold spices it's cooked with.

In contrast, stews such as *Red-Braised Pork Belly* (Hong Shao Rou) offer a deeper, slowly developed flavor profile. Here, the pork belly is simmered in a mixture of soy sauce, sugar, and a variety of spices, including star anise and cinnamon, until it reaches a melt-in-your-mouth tenderness that belies its spicy undertones.

Creating these dishes at home is an adventure in balancing the elements of flavor and heat. It's about understanding how the piquancy of chili interacts with the richness of pork and how the slow simmer of a stew can transform the straightforward into the sublime. These recipes invite you to explore the fiery side of Chinese cuisine, one sizzling dish at a time.

8.3.1 TWICE-COOKED PORK (HUI GUO ROU)

SZECHUAN TWICE-COOKED PORK BELLY

Preparation Time: 20 min

Cooking Time: 1 hr 10 min
Mode of Cooking: Boiling and Stir-Frying

Servings: 4

Ingredients: ●1 lb pork belly, skin on ●2 Tbsp vegetable oil ●4 cloves garlic, minced ●1 Tbsp ginger, minced ●2 leeks, sliced ●2 Tbsp bean paste ●1 Tbsp soy sauce ●1 Tbsp Shaoxing wine ●1 tsp sugar ●1 Tbsp chili oil ●½ tsp Szechuan peppercorns, crushed ●Salt to taste

Directions: ●Boil pork belly in water for about 1 hr or until tender ●Remove, cool, and slice thinly ●Heat vegetable oil in a wok, stir-fry garlic, ginger, and leeks until fragrant ●Add bean paste, stir-fry for 2 min. ●Add pork slices, stir-fry for 3 min. ●Stir in soy sauce, Shaoxing wine, sugar, chili oil, and Szechuan peppercorns, cook for another 5 min. ●Season with salt, serve hot

Tips: ●Use a cleaver for thinly slicing the pork for authentic texture ●Szechuan peppercorns can be adjusted for heat preference ●Serve with steamed rice for a complete meal

Nutritional Values: Calories: 630, Fat: 60g, Carbs: 4g, Protein: 22g, Sugar: 2g

FUJIAN STYLE TWICE-COOKED PORK

Preparation Time: 15 min

Cooking Time: 1 hr 15 min

Mode of Cooking: Boiling and Stir-Frying

Servings: 4

Ingredients: ●1 lb pork tenderloin ●1 Tbsp peanut oil ●3 Tbsp ketchup ●1 Tbsp hoisin sauce ●2 tsp dark soy sauce ●1 tsp light soy sauce ●1 Tbsp rice vinegar ●1 tsp honey ●3 green onions, chopped ●1 red bell pepper, cut into strips ●1 yellow bell pepper, cut into strips ●Salt and pepper to taste

Directions: ●Boil pork tenderloin in seasoned water until tender, about 1 hr ●Let cool, then cut into bite-sized pieces ●Heat peanut oil in a wok, stir-fry pork pieces until they begin to brown ●Mix ketchup, hoisin sauce, dark and light soy sauces, rice vinegar, and honey in a bowl ●Add sauce to the wok, stirring to coat pork evenly ●Add green onions and bell peppers, stir-fry for an additional 5 min. ●Season with salt and pepper

Tips: ●Mixing the sauce beforehand ensures even flavor distribution ●Can be served over a bed of noodles or rice for a satisfying dish ●Adjust the amount of honey to balance the sweetness and tanginess according to your taste

Nutritional Values: Calories: 320, Fat: 10g, Carbs: 20g, Protein: 35g, Sugar: 12g

HUNAN SMOKED PORK WITH LEEKS

Preparation Time: 25 min

Cooking Time: 55 min

Mode of Cooking: Boiling and Stir-Frying

Servings: 4

Ingredients: ●1.5 lbs smoked pork belly, thinly sliced ●2 Tbsp sesame oil ●3 leeks, cleaned and cut into 2-inch pieces ●2 Tbsp fermented black beans, rinsed and mashed ●1 Tbsp chili paste ●2 tsp minced garlic ●1 Tbsp soy sauce ●2 Tbsp vinegar ●1 tsp sugar ●Salt to taste

Directions: ●Boil smoked pork belly slices in water for 20 min to reduce saltiness, drain ●Heat sesame oil in a wok and stir-fry leeks until soft ●Add fermented black beans, chili paste, and garlic, stir-fry for 2 min. ●Add boiled pork, soy sauce, vinegar, and sugar, stir well and cook for 10 min. ●Season with salt to taste●Serve hot

Tips: ●Soaking smoked pork in hot water before cooking can help remove excess salt ●Fermented black beans add an umami depth to the dish not found in regular beans ●Perfect with a side of fluffy white rice to soak up the sauce

Nutritional Values: Calories: 540, Fat: 48g, Carbs: 8g, Protein: 24g, Sugar: 3g

8.3.2 MAPO TOFU WITH MINCED PORK

HUNAN SPICY MINCED PORK

Preparation Time: 15 min

Cooking Time: 25 min

Mode of Cooking: Stir-Frying

Servings: 4

Ingredients: ●450g minced pork ●2 Tbsp vegetable oil ●4 cloves garlic, minced ●2 Tbsp fresh ginger, minced ●1 red bell pepper, diced ●1 green bell pepper, diced ●4 spring onions, sliced ●2 Tbsp soy sauce ●3 Tbsp black bean sauce ●1 Tbsp rice vinegar ●1 tsp chili flakes ●1 Tbsp honey ●2 tsp Szechuan peppercorns, crushed ●Salt to taste ●Cooked white rice for serving

Directions: ●Heat oil in a large wok over medium-high heat ●Add garlic and ginger; stir-fry until fragrant, about 1 min ●Add minced pork; break it apart with a spatula and cook until browned, about 5 mins ●Stir in red and green bell peppers; cook for another 3-4 mins ●Add spring onions, soy sauce, black bean sauce, rice vinegar, chili flakes, honey, and Szechuan peppercorns; toss well to combine ●Cook for an additional 5-7 mins, until everything is well-cooked and the sauce has thickened slightly ●Serve hot over cooked rice

Tips: ●Use lean minced pork for less fat ●For a vegetarian version, substitute minced pork with tofu or tempeh ●Adjust chili flakes according to desired spice level

Nutritional Values: Calories: 350, Fat: 20g, Carbs: 15g, Protein: 28g, Sugar: 5g

SICHUAN PORK AND GREEN BEAN STIR-FRY

Preparation Time: 20 min
Cooking Time: 20 min
Mode of Cooking: Stir-Frying
Servings: 4
Ingredients: ●500g minced pork ●2 Tbsp sesame oil ●300g green beans, trimmed ●3 Tbsp Sichuan bean paste ●1 Tbsp ginger, minced ●3 cloves garlic, minced ●1 Tbsp Sichuan peppercorns ●2 Tbsp soy sauce ●1 Tbsp Shaoxing wine ●1 tsp sugar ●Salt to taste ●2 Tbsp scallions, finely chopped for garnish ●Cooked white rice for serving

Directions: ●Heat sesame oil in a wok over medium heat ●Add Sichuan peppercorns and toast until fragrant; remove and crush ●In the same wok, add minced pork, cooking until it starts to brown, about 7-8 mins ●Add ginger and garlic, stir-fry for 2 mins ●Introduce green beans and cook until they are bright green and tender, about 5 mins ●Stir in Sichuan bean paste, soy sauce, Shaoxing wine, sugar, and crushed peppercorns, cooking for another 5 mins ●Season with

salt and mix well ●Garnish with scallions and serve over rice

Tips: ●Toast Sichuan peppercorns before crushing to enhance their aroma ●Green beans should remain slightly crunchy for texture ●Substitute Shaoxing wine with dry sherry if necessary

Nutritional Values: Calories: 380, Fat: 22g, Carbs: 12g, Protein: 30g, Sugar: 4g

GINGER PORK BELLY WITH CRISPY LOTUS ROOT

Preparation Time: 30 min
Cooking Time: 1 hr
Mode of Cooking: Roasting
Servings: 4
Ingredients: ●700g pork belly, sliced ●200g lotus root, sliced thinly ●2 Tbsp grated ginger ●4 Tbsp soy sauce ●2 Tbsp oyster sauce ●1 Tbsp honey ●2 cloves garlic, minced ●1 tsp five-spice powder ●2 Tbsp vegetable oil ●Salt and pepper to taste ●Green onions, sliced for garnish

Directions: ●Preheat oven to 375°F (190°C) ●In a bowl, mix soy sauce, oyster sauce, honey, ginger, garlic, and five-spice powder to create marinade ●Toss pork belly slices in the marinade and let sit for 20 mins ●In a separate bowl, toss lotus root slices with vegetable oil, salt, and pepper ●Arrange pork belly and lotus root slices on a baking tray lined with parchment paper ●Roast in the oven for about 40-45 mins, turning halfway through, until pork is crispy and lotus root is golden ●Garnish with green onions before serving

Tips: ●Marinate pork belly for longer to intensify flavors ●Lotus root can be found in Asian markets; it adds a crunchy texture ●Pair with jasmine rice to balance the dish's rich flavors

Nutritional Values: Calories: 580, Fat: 44g, Carbs: 22g, Protein: 25g, Sugar: 8g

CHAPTER 9: BEEF BLISS

9.1 BEEF STIR-FRIES AND NOODLE DISHES

In the dynamic world of Chinese cuisine, beef stir-fries and noodle dishes stand out for their robust flavors and satisfying textures, offering a hearty meal that combines the rich depth of beef with the comforting familiarity of noodles. These dishes, varied and versatile, reflect the culinary diversity found across China, from the bustling streets of Beijing to the quiet hills of Guilin.

Beef stir-fries are all about the sizzle and speed of the wok. A dish like *Mongolian Beef,* for instance, showcases thinly sliced beef quickly cooked with onions and scallions in a savory, slightly sweet sauce enhanced with soy and hoisin. The key is the intense heat that sears the beef, locking in juices and flavor, while the vegetables remain crisp and vibrant.

Transitioning to noodles, dishes such as *Beef Chow Fun* offer a different textural experience. Here, wide rice noodles slide through the wok, picking up hints of smoke from the high heat, their chewiness complementing the tender slices of beef and crunchy bean sprouts. This dish epitomizes the balance that Chinese cooking strives for—not just in flavors but in the play of textures and colors.

Exploring these beef recipes allows home cooks to dive into the quick, fiery world of the Chinese kitchen, mastering the rapid moves of stir-frying or the gentle toss of noodles. Each dish not only satisfies the appetite but also invites a deeper appreciation for the traditions that have shaped these beloved recipes.

9.1.1 MONGOLIAN BEEF

MONGOLIAN BEEF WITH BLACK BEAN SAUCE

Preparation Time: 10 min
Cooking Time: 20 min
Mode of Cooking: Stir-Frying
Servings: 4
Ingredients: ●1 lb. flank steak, thinly sliced against the grain ●2 Tbsp vegetable oil ●1 red bell pepper, julienned ●1 green bell pepper, julienned ●2 cloves garlic, minced ●1 inch ginger, minced ●For the sauce: 2 Tbsp fermented black beans, rinsed and mashed ●1 Tbsp soy sauce ●1 Tbsp hoisin sauce ●1 tsp sugar ●½ cup water ●1 Tbsp cornstarch dissolved in 2 Tbsp water

Directions: ●Marinate the beef slices in a mixture of soy sauce and cornstarch for 10 min ●Heat oil in a wok over high heat and stir-fry beef until browned and almost cooked, then set aside ●In the same wok, add a bit more oil if needed, and stir-fry garlic, ginger, and bell peppers for 2-3 min ●Add the mashed black beans, soy sauce, hoisin sauce, sugar, and water to the wok, bringing to a simmer ●Return the beef to the wok, add the cornstarch mixture to thicken the sauce, stir well until the beef is coated and the sauce is glossy ●Serve immediately

Tips: ●Marinate the beef ahead of time for extra tenderness ●Use fresh black beans for a more authentic flavor ●Adjust the amount of sugar based on your preference

Nutritional Values: Calories: 298, Fat: 17g, Carbs: 13g, Protein: 24g, Sugar: 5g

SZECHUAN BEEF STIR-FRY

Preparation Time: 15 min

Cooking Time: 10 min

Mode of Cooking: Stir-Frying

Servings: 4

Ingredients: ●1 lb. beef sirloin, thinly sliced ●2 Tbsp sesame oil ●3 Tbsp Szechuan peppercorns, crushed ●1 Tbsp chili flakes ●1 Tbsp garlic, minced ●1 Tbsp ginger, minced ●1 red onion, sliced ●1 cup snap peas ●For the sauce: 3 Tbsp soy sauce ●2 Tbsp oyster sauce ●1 Tbsp rice vinegar ●1 Tbsp brown sugar ●1 tsp cornstarch mixed with 1 Tbsp water

Directions: ●Toast Szechuan peppercorns and chili flakes in a dry pan until fragrant ●Heat sesame oil in a wok, add garlic, ginger, and beef, stir-frying until beef is just cooked ●Add red onion and snap peas, stir-fry for additional 2-3 min ●Mix sauce ingredients together and pour over the beef mixture, cooking until the sauce thickens slightly and coats the ingredients ●Serve hot with rice or noodles

Tips: ●Use a very hot wok to seal the flavors and juices of the beef ●Adjust chili flakes according to spice preference ●Toasting Szechuan peppercorns before use intensifies their unique numbing sensation

Nutritional Values: Calories: 325, Fat: 19g, Carbs: 14g, Protein: 26g, Sugar: 6g

BEEF AND BROCCOLI WITH GARLIC SAUCE

Preparation Time: 20 min

Cooking Time: 15 min

Mode of Cooking: Stir-Frying

Servings: 4

Ingredients: ●1 lb. beef tenderloin, cut into strips ●3 Tbsp vegetable oil ●4 cups broccoli florets ●2 Tbsp garlic, minced ●1 Tbsp ginger, minced ●For the garlic sauce: ¼ cup soy sauce ●1 Tbsp hoisin sauce ●2 tsp sesame oil ●2 tsp sugar ●½ cup beef broth ●1 tsp cornstarch dissolved in 1 Tbsp water

Directions: ●Marinate beef in a mixture of soy sauce and sesame oil for 15 min ●Heat 2 Tbsp oil in a wok and stir-fry beef until it's browned but still tender, remove and set aside ●Using the same wok, add the remaining oil, and stir-fry broccoli for 5 min until

vibrant and tender-crisp ●Add garlic and ginger, stir-frying for another minute until fragrant ●Reintroduce beef to the wok, pour in garlic sauce mixture, and bring to a simmer until the sauce thickens and evenly coats the beef and broccoli ●Serve immediately over a bed of jasmine rice

Tips: ●Blanching broccoli before stir-frying can help retain its green color ●Adjust the amount of garlic in the sauce to taste ●Dissolving cornstarch in water before adding helps prevent clumping for a smoother sauce

Nutritional Values: Calories: 270, Fat: 14g, Carbs: 13g, Protein: 25g, Sugar: 4g

9.1.2 BEEF CHOW FUN

CLASSIC BEEF CHOW FUN

Preparation Time: 15 min

Cooking Time: 10 min

Mode of Cooking: Stir-frying

Servings: 4

Ingredients: ●400g flat rice noodles ●300g sliced beef (flank steak or sirloin) ●1 Tbsp soy sauce for marinade ●1 tsp cornstarch for marinade ●2 Tbsp vegetable oil ●1 Tbsp minced garlic ●1 Tbsp minced ginger ●1 cup bean sprouts ●2 scallions, cut into 2-inch pieces ●2 Tbsp oyster sauce ●1 Tbsp dark soy sauce ●2 tsp sesame oil ●Salt and pepper to taste

Directions: ●Combine beef slices with soy sauce and cornstarch for marinade and let it sit for 10 min ●Heat oil in a wok or large skillet over high heat until shimmering ●Add minced garlic and ginger, stir-fry for 30 seconds until fragrant ●Add marinated beef to the wok, spreading it out and sear without moving for 1 min, then stir-fry until it's about 80% cooked, remove and set aside ●In the same wok, add flat rice noodles, oyster sauce, and dark soy sauce, tossing continuously to prevent sticking, for about 2 min ●Return beef to wok, add bean sprouts and scallions, stir-fry everything together for another 2 min ●Finish with a drizzle of sesame oil, salt, and pepper to taste, toss well and serve immediately

Tips: ●Slice beef against the grain for tenderness ●Use a well-seasoned wok to achieve the 'wok hei' (wok's breath) flavor ●Rinse flat rice noodles under warm water to prevent sticking and ease stir-frying

Nutritional Values: Calories: 520, Fat: 15g, Carbs: 70g, Protein: 25g, Sugar: 3g

SPICY SICHUAN BEEF CHOW FUN

Preparation Time: 20 min

Cooking Time: 15 min

Mode of Cooking: Stir-frying

Servings: 4

Ingredients: ●400g flat rice noodles ●300g sliced beef (rib eye or brisket) ●2 Tbsp Sichuan chili oil ●1 tsp Sichuan peppercorns, crushed ●1 Tbsp soy sauce for marinade ●1 tsp cornstarch for marinade ●2 Tbsp vegetable oil ●3 cloves garlic, minced ●3 Tbsp spicy bean paste ●1 red bell pepper, sliced ●1 green bell pepper, sliced ●1 onion, sliced ●1 tsp sugar ●2 Tbsp light soy sauce ●1 Tbsp sesame oil ●Salt to taste

Directions: ●Marinate beef slices in soy sauce and cornstarch, set aside for 15 min ●Heat Sichuan chili oil in wok over medium heat, add Sichuan peppercorns and garlic, stir-fry until fragrant ●Increase heat, add marinated beef and stir-fry until browned, remove beef and set aside ●In the same wok, add spicy bean paste, bell peppers, and onion, stir-fry for 5 min ●Return beef to the wok, add flat rice noodles, sugar, and light soy sauce, toss well to combine ●Cook for another 5 min, adjust seasoning with salt, drizzle sesame oil, and serve hot

Tips: ●Work in batches if your wok is not large enough to prevent overcrowding and ensure even cooking ●Immediately serve to enjoy the crunchiness of the peppers and the tender beef ●Adjust the level of spicy bean paste to control the heat according to your preference

Nutritional Values: Calories: 580, Fat: 22g, Carbs: 68g, Protein: 28g, Sugar: 5g

BEEF AND BROCCOLI CHOW FUN

Preparation Time: 25 min

Cooking Time: 20 min

Mode of Cooking: Stir-frying

Servings: 4

Ingredients: ●400g flat rice noodles ●300g beef slices (top round) ●1 cup broccoli florets, blanched ●2 Tbsp oyster sauce ●1 Tbsp soy sauce for marinade ●1 tsp cornstarch for marinade ●2 Tbsp vegetable oil ●2 garlic cloves, minced ●1 Tbsp ginger, minced ●1/4 cup beef broth ●2 tsp cornstarch mixed with 2 Tbsp water for slurry ●1 Tbsp hoisin sauce ●1 tsp sesame oil ●Salt and pepper to taste

Directions: ●Marinate beef slices in soy sauce and cornstarch, let it rest for 15 min ●Heat vegetable oil in a wok over high heat, add garlic and ginger, stir-fry until aromatic ●Add marinated beef and stir-fry until it's no longer pink, remove and set aside ●In the same wok, add broccoli and beef broth, cover and steam for 3 min ●Uncover, return beef to the wok, add flat rice noodles, oyster sauce, and hoisin sauce, toss to combine everything well ●Thicken sauce with cornstarch slurry, cook for another 2 min until the sauce coats the noodles and ingredients ●Season with sesame oil, salt, and pepper before serving

Tips: ●Blanch broccoli in boiling water for 2 min to retain its vibrant green color and crisp texture ●Add the cornstarch slurry gradually to prevent the sauce from becoming too thick ●Use freshly ground pepper to enhance flavor

Nutritional Values: Calories: 560, Fat: 18g, Carbs: 72g, Protein: 27g, Sugar: 4g

9.2 BRAISED BEEF AND HOT POT

Braised beef and hot pot are not just methods of cooking but are revered traditions within Chinese culinary culture, each serving as a hearty centerpiece at family gatherings and festive celebrations. These dishes draw out the richness of beef through slow-cooking processes that emphasize depth of flavor and tenderness of meat.

In braising, pieces of beef are seared to develop a complex flavor base and then slowly cooked in a mixture of broth, soy sauce, star anise, and other spices. This method, exemplified in dishes like *Chinese Braised Beef Shank*, transforms tougher cuts into melt-in-your-mouth delicacies that are both succulent and aromatic. The slow simmering not only softens the meat but also infuses it with the flavors of the braising liquid, creating a harmonious blend that is deeply satisfying.

The hot pot, on the other hand, is an interactive dining experience that brings people together around a bubbling pot of broth. Diners cook thin slices of beef and a variety of other ingredients at the table, enjoying the social aspect as much as the culinary one. The broth, enriched with each addition, becomes a flavorful soup that is as unique as the company sharing the meal.

Engaging with these cooking styles offers a window into the patience required in traditional Chinese cooking and the communal spirit that these meals foster. Each dish is a celebration of flavor, a testament to the culinary lore that has seasoned these techniques for generations.

9.2.1 CHINESE BRAISED BEEF SHANK

ANHUI-STYLE BRAISED BEEF SHANK

Preparation Time: 20 min

Cooking Time: 2 hr

Mode of Cooking: Braising

Servings: 4

Ingredients: ●2 lb. beef shank ●1 Tbsp. Sichuan peppercorns ●2 star anise pods ●3 Chinese dried red chili peppers ●¼ cup Shaoxing wine ●3 Tbsp. light soy sauce ●2 Tbsp. dark soy sauce ●1 Tbsp. rock sugar ●5 slices of ginger ●4 cloves of garlic, smashed ●2 scallions, chopped into 2-inch pieces ●Water to cover

Directions: ●Blanch beef shank in boiling water for 5 minutes then drain ●Heat a clean pot over medium heat and add the beef shank back in along with Sichuan peppercorns, star anise, dried chili peppers, Shaoxing wine, light and dark soy sauce, rock sugar, ginger, garlic, and scallions ●Add enough water to cover the beef shank ●Bring to a boil, then reduce heat to low, cover, and simmer for 2 hours until the beef is tender ●Slice the beef shank and serve with some of the braising liquid as a sauce

Tips: ●Slice beef against the grain to enhance tenderness ●Skim off any fat from the surface of the braising liquid before serving for a clearer sauce ●Serve with steamed bok choy for a complete meal

Nutritional Values: Calories: 450, Fat: 14g, Carbs: 10g, Protein: 68g, Sugar: 4g

FUJIAN RED WINE BRAISED BEEF SHANK

Preparation Time: 25 min

Cooking Time: 3 hr

Mode of Cooking: Braising

Servings: 6

Ingredients: ●3 lb. beef shank ●½ cup Fujian red rice wine ●¼ cup light soy sauce ●2 Tbsp. dark soy sauce ●1 Tbsp. sugar ●6 cups water ●2 inches ginger, sliced ●5 cloves garlic, whole ●1 white onion, quartered ●2 star anise ●1 cinnamon stick ●3 bay leaves ●Salt to taste

Directions: ●Marinate beef shank with light soy sauce, dark soy sauce, and Fujian red rice wine for 15 minutes ●In a large pot, bring water to a boil and add the marinated beef shank along with ginger, garlic, onion, star anise, cinnamon stick, bay leaves, and sugar ●Return to a boil, then reduce heat to a simmer, cover, and cook for 3 hours until beef is very tender ●Season with salt to taste before serving

Tips: ●The longer marination time enhances the beef's flavor ●Use a piece of cheesecloth to wrap the spices for easy removal if desired ●Leftover braising liquid can be used as a base for soup

Nutritional Values: Calories: 510, Fat: 18g, Carbs: 15g, Protein: 75g, Sugar: 6g

HUNAN SPICY BRAISED BEEF SHANK

Preparation Time: 15 min

Cooking Time: 2.5 hr

Mode of Cooking: Braising

Servings: 4

Ingredients: ●2 lb. beef shank ●2 Tbsp. chili bean paste (Doubanjiang) ●¼ cup rice wine ●3 Tbsp. soy sauce ●1 Tbsp. sugar ●5 cups water ●3 Tbsp. vegetable oil ●5 cloves garlic, minced ●2 inches ginger, minced

- 1 green bell pepper, diced •1 red bell pepper, diced •2 scallions, sliced

Directions: •Heat vegetable oil in a large pot over medium flame and sauté garlic, ginger, and chili bean paste until fragrant •Add beef shank, rice wine, soy sauce, sugar, and water •Bring to a boil, reduce heat to low, cover, and simmer for 2.5 hours until beef is tender •During the last 30 minutes of cooking, add diced bell peppers and simmer uncovered •Garnish with scallions before serving

Tips: •Roasting the beef shank before braising can add depth to the dish's flavor •Adjust the amount of chili bean paste to control the spiciness according to taste •This dish is ideally served with white rice to balance the flavors

Nutritional Values: Calories: 470, Fat: 20g, Carbs: 12g, Protein: 60g, Sugar: 5g

9.2.2 SICHUAN BEEF HOT POT

TRADITIONAL SICHUAN BEEF HOT POT

Preparation Time: 30 min
Cooking Time: 2 hr
Mode of Cooking: Simmer
Servings: 4
Ingredients: •1 lb. beef brisket, thinly sliced •4 cups beef broth •1 cup Sichuan spicy hot pot base •2 Tbsp soy sauce •1 Tbsp Sichuan peppercorns •2 star anise •1 cinnamon stick •3 slices ginger •2 cloves garlic, smashed •1 Tbsp doubanjiang (fermented broad bean chili paste) •2 cups napa cabbage, chopped •1 cup daikon radish, sliced •8 oz. tofu, cubed •4 oz. enoki mushrooms •2 green onions, chopped •Cooking oil for frying

Directions: •Heat oil in a large pot over medium heat •Add Sichuan peppercorns, star anise, cinnamon stick, slices of ginger, and smashed garlic cloves; cook until fragrant •Stir in doubanjiang to blend with the spices •Pour in beef broth and Sichuan spicy hot pot base; bring to a boil •Add sliced beef brisket, reduce heat to simmer; cook for 1.5 hr •Add napa cabbage, daikon radish, tofu, and enoki mushrooms into the pot; simmer for an additional 20 min •Garnish with chopped green onions

Tips: •Serve with a side of steamed rice or dipping sauces for added flavor •Avoid overcooking the enoki mushrooms to maintain their texture

Nutritional Values: Calories: 420, Fat: 25g, Carbs: 12g, Protein: 35g, Sugar: 3g

SICHUAN BEEF TALLOW HOT POT

Preparation Time: 35 min
Cooking Time: 2 hr 30 min
Mode of Cooking: Simmer
Servings: 6
Ingredients: •1.5 lb. beef slices •6 cups water •½ cup beef tallow •¼ cup Sichuan peppercorns •2 Tbsp chili flakes •1 Tbsp black bean paste •5 slices ginger •4 cloves garlic, minced •1 leek, cut into sections •1 bunch cilantro, chopped •1 Tbsp doubanjiang •2 Tbsp Shaoxing wine •2 star anise •1 cinnamon stick •Vegetables (bok choy, lotus root, mushrooms) and noodles for serving

Directions: •Melt beef tallow in a hot pot or a heavy-bottomed pot over medium heat •Add Sichuan peppercorns, chili flakes, and whole spices; cook until aromatic •Stir in ginger, garlic, leek, and black bean paste; fry for a couple of minutes until fragrant •Pour in water, doubanjiang, and Shaoxing wine; bring to a boil, then lower the heat and simmer for 2 hours •Skim off any foam that arises •Add beef slices and cook until they are just done •Serve hot pot with fresh vegetables and noodles on the side

Tips: •Skim the broth regularly to keep it clear •Use thinly sliced beef for quick cooking •Serve with additional Sichuan pepper oil for extra heat

Nutritional Values: Calories: 480, Fat: 30g, Carbs: 10g, Protein: 40g, Sugar: 5g

FIERY SICHUAN BROTH HOT POT

Preparation Time: 20 min
Cooking Time: 1 hr 30 min
Mode of Cooking: Simmer
Servings: 5
Ingredients: •1 lb. beef shank, thinly sliced •4 cups chicken stock •3 cups water •½ cup homemade chili oil •¼ cup light soy sauce •3 Tbsp Pixian bean paste •2 bay leaves •1 Tbsp whole Sichuan peppercorns •2 star anise •1 cinnamon stick •1 black cardamom •4 dried red chilies •5 slices ginger •3 cloves garlic,

crushed •Assorted vegetables (cabbage, spinach) and mushrooms for serving

Directions: •Combine chicken stock, water, chili oil, soy sauce, and Pixian bean paste in a pot over medium heat •Add bay leaves, Sichuan peppercorns, star anise, cinnamon, black cardamom, dried chilies, ginger, and garlic; bring to a boil and simmer for 1 hr •Add thinly sliced beef shank and simmer for about 20-30 min or until tender •Serve hot with assorted vegetables and mushrooms

Tips: •Use a fine mesh when serving to avoid eating the whole spices •Adjust the chili oil according to your spice tolerance •You can add noodles at the end for a heartier meal

Nutritional Values: Calories: 310, Fat: 18g, Carbs: 8g, Protein: 28g, Sugar: 2g

9.3 BEEF SOUPS AND BROTHS

The warmth of a simmering pot of beef soup or broth permeates the kitchen with an inviting aroma that promises both comfort and nourishment. In Chinese culinary tradition, beef soups and broths are not just food; they are a form of art that requires patience and precision, embodying the philosophy of warming the body and soul through careful, slow cooking.

Each region in China brings its own character to these dishes, from the spice-laden broths of the Sichuan province to the subtle, anise-flavored soups of the north. A standout among these is the *Niurou Mian*, or beef noodle soup, a beloved dish that combines chewy noodles with succulent pieces of beef, stewed in a broth richly flavored with soy sauce, star anise, and cinnamon. The broth, often simmered for hours, transforms the beef into tender morsels that melt in the mouth, while absorbing the aromatic complexity of the spices.

Preparing these soups at home is an exercise in mindfulness, as each ingredient is added at just the right time to achieve the perfect harmony of flavors. The slow simmer allows the ingredients to meld together, creating a broth that is rich, deep, and thoroughly infused with essence.

This journey through beef soups and broths not only satisfies the stomach but also teaches the virtue of patience, as the slow process unfolds into a rewarding culinary experience that soothes and revitalizes.

9.3.1 CLEAR BEEF BROTH WITH RADISH AND TOFU

CLEAR BEEF BROTH WITH RADISH AND TOFU

Preparation Time: 20 min
Cooking Time: 1 hr 30 min
Mode of Cooking: Simmer
Servings: 4

Ingredients: •1 lb. beef shank •8 cups water •2 medium daikon radish, peeled and quartered •1 block firm tofu, cubed •3 slices ginger •2 scallions, chopped •1 Tbsp soy sauce •Salt to taste •1 tsp sesame oil •Cilantro for garnish

Directions: •Bring the water to a boil in a large pot •Add the beef shank and let it boil for 10 minutes then remove the foam that rises to the top •Add ginger slices and half of the scallions •Reduce heat to low and simmer for 1 hr •Remove the beef shank and set aside to cool, then slice thinly •Add daikon radish to the broth and simmer until tender, about 20 min •Add tofu, soy sauce, and salt adjusting the seasoning to taste, cook for an additional 5 min •Serve hot garnished with sliced beef, remaining scallions, cilantro, and a drizzle of sesame oil

Tips: •Use a fine mesh skimmer to remove impurities for a clearer broth •For a fuller flavor, you could simmer the broth with the beef shank longer, up to 2 hrs •Chill the broth overnight to easily skim off any fat that solidifies on the surface

Nutritional Values: Calories: 220, Fat: 10g, Carbs: 8g, Protein: 26g, Sugar: 3g

BEEF AND GOJI BERRY BROTH

Preparation Time: 15 min

Cooking Time: 2 hr

Mode of Cooking: Simmer

Servings: 4

Ingredients: ●1.5 lbs beef bones ●10 cups water ●½ cup goji berries ●1 large carrot, sliced ●1 piece of ginger, 3 inches, sliced ●Salt to taste ●2 Tbsp rice wine ●4 green onions, chopped

Directions: ●Place beef bones in a large pot and cover with water ●Bring to a boil and skim off any foam that forms ●Reduce heat, add ginger, salt, and rice wine, then cover and simmer for 1.5 hrs ●Add carrots and goji berries, and simmer for another 30 min ●Strain the broth, discarding the solids ●Serve the clear broth sprinkled with green onions

Tips: ●Goji berries add not only a unique flavor but also are packed with antioxidants ●Soak goji berries in warm water for 10 min before adding to the broth to soften them ●Roasting bones before simmering can add depth to the broth's flavor

Nutritional Values: Calories: 150, Fat: 4g, Carbs: 10g, Protein: 18g, Sugar: 6g

BOK CHOY AND BEEF CLEAR SOUP

Preparation Time: 10 min

Cooking Time: 25 min

Mode of Cooking: Boil

Servings: 4

Ingredients: ●1 lb. thinly sliced beef sirloin ●8 cups beef broth ●4 baby bok choy, quartered ●2 Tbsp soy sauce ●1 tsp white pepper ●2 tsp sesame oil ●4 slices ginger ●Salt to taste ●2 scallions, finely sliced

Directions: ●Bring the beef broth to a simmer in a large pot ●Add ginger slices and soy sauce ●Add beef slices and cook until they are just done, about 2-3 min ●Add bok choy and simmer until tender, about 5 min ●Season with white pepper, salt, and drizzle with sesame oil ●Serve hot, garnished with scallions

Tips: ●Slicing the beef thinly allows it to cook quickly and stay tender ●Bok choy can be replaced with other greens like spinach or watercress for variation ●Adjust soy sauce and sesame oil quantities to suit your taste for a more personalized broth

Nutritional Values: Calories: 175, Fat: 7g, Carbs: 3g, Protein: 24g, Sugar: 2g

9.3.2 SPICY BEEF NOODLE SOUP (NIUROU MIAN)

SICHUAN SPICY BEEF NOODLE SOUP

Preparation Time: 30 min

Cooking Time: 2 hrs

Mode of Cooking: Stovetop

Servings: 4

Ingredients: ●1 lb. beef shank ●2 Tbsp Sichuan peppercorns ●3 star anise ●1 cinnamon stick ●4 cloves garlic, smashed ●3 slices ginger ●2 Tbsp spicy bean paste ●8 cups beef broth ●1 Tbsp soy sauce ●1 Tbsp rice wine ●2 tsp sugar ●4 servings fresh wheat noodles ●2 scallions, thinly sliced ●1 cup bok choy, chopped ●Chili oil for garnish

Directions: ●Toast Sichuan peppercorns, star anise, and cinnamon in a pot over medium heat until fragrant ●Add garlic, ginger, and spicy bean paste, sautéing until aromatic ●Pour in beef broth, add beef shank, and bring to a boil ●Skim off any foam that rises to the top ●Add soy sauce, rice wine, and sugar, simmering on low heat for 1.5 hr or until beef is tender ●Cook noodles according to package instructions and divide among bowls ●Slice beef and place over noodles, adding bok choy to the hot soup to lightly cook ●Pour broth over, garnish with scallions and a drizzle of chili oil

Tips: ●If beef shank is not available, brisket makes a good alternative ●For a less spicy soup, adjust the amount of spicy bean paste to taste

Nutritional Values: Calories: 610, Fat: 20g, Carbs: 68g, Protein: 34g, Sugar: 5g

BEIJING-STYLE BRAISED BEEF NOODLE SOUP

Preparation Time: 20 min

Cooking Time: 3 hrs

Mode of Cooking: Stovetop

Servings: 6

Ingredients: ●1.5 lbs. beef brisket, cut into chunks ●2 Tbsp vegetable oil ●1 onion, chopped ●3 cloves garlic, minced ●1 inch ginger, minced ●5 star anise ●2 Tbsp Chinese five spice powder ●3 Tbsp light soy sauce ●2 Tbsp dark soy sauce ●1/4 cup Chinese Shaoxing wine

●6 cups water ●3 large carrots, cut into thick slices ●1 lb. fresh thick wheat noodles ●1 bunch cilantro, for garnish ●2 green onions, chopped, for garnish

Directions: ●Heat oil in a large pot over medium-high heat, brown beef brisket on all sides ●Remove beef and set aside ●In the same pot, add onion, garlic, and ginger, cooking until softened ●Return beef to pot with star anise, Chinese five spice, soy sauces, Shaoxing wine, and water ●Bring to a boil, then reduce heat to low, cover, and simmer for 2.5 hrs until beef is tender ●Add carrots in the last 30 min of cooking ●Cook noodles according to package directions ●Serve soup with noodles, garnished with cilantro and green onions

Tips: ●To enhance the flavor, let the soup sit for a few hours or overnight before serving ●Use a fine mesh strainer to skim off any fat that rises to the top for a clearer broth

Nutritional Values: Calories: 520, Fat: 16g, Carbs: 56g, Protein: 35g, Sugar: 4g

TAIWANESE BEEF NOODLE SOUP

Preparation Time: 25 min
Cooking Time: 8 hrs (Slow Cooker)
Mode of Cooking: Slow Cooker
Servings: 4

Ingredients: ●2 lbs. beef short ribs ●1/4 cup soy sauce ●3 Tbsp rock sugar ●1/4 cup tomato paste ●2 star anise ●1 cinnamon stick ●4 slices ginger ●4 cloves garlic, minced ●5 cups beef broth ●3 Tbsp rice wine vinegar ●2 Tbsp chili paste ●1 lb. fresh, thin wheat noodles ●1 bunch baby bok choy, quartered ●Pickled mustard greens, for garnish

Directions: ●Combine beef short ribs, soy sauce, rock sugar, tomato paste, star anise, cinnamon, ginger, garlic, beef broth, rice wine vinegar, and chili paste in a slow cooker ●Cook on low heat for 8 hrs until beef is very tender and falls off the bone ●In the last 30 min of cooking, add baby bok choy to the slow cooker to wilt ●Cook noodles according to package instructions and divide among bowls ●Place a portion of beef on noodles, ladle broth and bok choy over, and garnish with pickled mustard greens

Tips: ●For a more intense flavor, sear the short ribs before adding them to the slow cooker ●Adjust chili paste according to spice preference

Nutritional Values: Calories: 630, Fat: 35g, Carbs: 45g, Protein: 38g, Sugar: 6g

CHAPTER 10: SEAFOOD SENSATIONS

10.1 STIR-FRIED SEAFOOD SPECIALTIES

Stir-fried seafood is a vibrant chapter in the story of Chinese cuisine, showcasing the country's expansive coastline and its relationship with the sea. Dishes such as Salt and Pepper Shrimp and Garlic Butter Lobster not only highlight the fresh catch of the day but also the skill with which it is enhanced through rapid, high-heat cooking methods.

In a typical stir-fry, the seafood is the star, with each piece quickly tossed in a flaming hot wok to seal in its delicate flavors. The key to perfect seafood stir-fry lies in the precise timing and the freshness of the ingredients. Garlic, ginger, and scallions often join the mix, adding a fragrant backdrop to the sweet and tender seafood. Meanwhile, splashes of soy sauce or a pinch of sugar balance the flavors, adding depth without overwhelming the natural taste of the ocean. This cooking style reflects the Chinese culinary principle of harmonizing flavors and textures, creating dishes that are complex in taste yet simple in appearance. The high heat preserves the seafood's succulent texture, while the quick tosses ensure that each morsel is evenly coated with the aromatic sauce, resulting in a dish that is both visually appealing and deeply satisfying.

Engaging in seafood stir-fry at home brings a piece of the sea into the kitchen, offering a quick, flavorful escape that pays homage to the traditional Chinese coastal kitchens, where the bounty of the sea is respected and celebrated in every dish.

10.1.1 SALT AND PEPPER SHRIMP

SALT AND PEPPER SHRIMP WITH A TWIST

Preparation Time: 15 min
Cooking Time: 10 min
Mode of Cooking: Stir-Frying
Servings: 4
Ingredients: ●1 lb. large shrimp, peeled and deveined ●1 tsp salt ●2 tsp Sichuan peppercorns, crushed ●1 Tbsp cornstarch ●2 Tbsp vegetable oil ●5 cloves garlic, minced ●1 green chili, thinly sliced ●3 green onions, sliced ●1 tsp soy sauce ●1 tsp sesame oil ●½ tsp sugar

Directions: ●Combine shrimp with salt, Sichuan peppercorns, and cornstarch in a bowl and mix well ●Heat oil in a wok over medium-high heat ●Add garlic and green chili to the wok and stir-fry until aromatic ●Add shrimp to the wok and stir-fry until they turn pink and are cooked through ●Stir in green onions, soy sauce, sesame oil, and sugar, and stir-fry for another minute

Tips: ●Use fresh shrimp for the best flavor and texture ●For extra heat, increase the amount of green chili according to your taste preference ●Ensure to continuously stir the shrimp while frying to prevent sticking and ensure even cooking

Nutritional Values: Calories: 230, Fat: 10g, Carbs: 6g, Protein: 31g, Sugar: 1g

GINGER SCALLION LOBSTER

Preparation Time: 20 min
Cooking Time: 12 min
Mode of Cooking: Stir-Frying
Servings: 4

Ingredients: ●2 whole lobsters (approx. 1.5 lb. each), chopped into pieces ●2 Tbsp ginger, minced ●3 Tbsp scallions, chopped ●1 Tbsp soy sauce ●2 tsp Shaoxing wine ●1 tsp sugar ●1 Tbsp vegetable oil ●1/2 tsp sesame oil ●Salt and pepper to taste

Directions: ●Blanch lobster pieces in boiling water for 1 min., then drain ●Heat oil in a wok over high heat ●Add ginger and half of the scallions, stir-frying until fragrant ●Add lobster pieces to the wok, season with salt and pepper, and stir-fry for about 5 mins ●Mix soy sauce, Shaoxing wine, and sugar in a small bowl and pour over the lobster, cooking for an additional 2 mins ●Drizzle with sesame oil and garnish with remaining scallions before serving

Tips: ●Do not overcook the lobster to maintain its succulent texture ●Use high heat for stir-frying to seal in flavors ●Shaoxing wine can be replaced with dry sherry if unavailable

Nutritional Values: Calories: 320, Fat: 8g, Carbs: 5g, Protein: 48g, Sugar: 1g

SZECHUAN SPICY OCTOPUS

Preparation Time: 25 min

Cooking Time: 15 min

Mode of Cooking: Stir-Frying

Servings: 4

Ingredients: ●1 lb. baby octopus, cleaned ●2 Tbsp Szechuan chili paste ●1 Tbsp soy sauce ●1 Tbsp ginger, minced ●3 garlic cloves, minced ●¼ cup chicken stock ●1 tsp sugar ●1 Tbsp vegetable oil ●2 tsp sesame seeds ●1 green onion, sliced ●Salt to taste

Directions: ●Marinate octopus with Szechuan chili paste, soy sauce, sugar, and salt for 15 mins ●Heat oil in a wok over medium-high heat ●Add ginger and garlic to the wok and stir-fry until aromatic ●Increase heat to high, add octopus, and stir-fry for about 2-3 mins ●Add chicken stock and cook for another 10 mins or until the octopus is tender ●Garnish with sesame seeds and green onion before serving

Tips: ●To ensure the octopus becomes tender, not chewy, avoid overcooking ●Szechuan chili paste can be adjusted based on spice preference ●Serve immediately for best taste

Nutritional Values: Calories: 180, Fat: 5g, Carbs: 8g, Protein: 25g, Sugar: 2g

10.1.2 GARLIC BUTTER LOBSTER

SICHUAN-STYLE GARLIC BUTTER LOBSTER

Preparation Time: 15 min

Cooking Time: 10 min

Mode of Cooking: Stir-Frying

Servings: 4

Ingredients: ●2 live lobsters, approximately 1.5 lb each, split and cleaned ●4 Tbsp unsalted butter ●4 cloves garlic, minced ●2 Tbsp ginger, minced ●3 Tbsp doubanjiang (fermented bean paste) ●1 Tbsp light soy sauce ●2 tsp sugar ●1 small bunch of green onions, sliced into 1-inch pieces ●1 tsp Sichuan peppercorns, ground ●1 Tbsp vegetable oil ●Salt to taste ●1 tsp sesame oil for finishing

Directions: ●Heat vegetable oil and 2 Tbsp butter in a wok or large skillet over medium heat ●Add garlic and ginger, stir-fry until aromatic about 2 mins ●Increase the heat to high, add lobster pieces, and stir-fry for 2-3 mins ●Add doubanjiang, light soy sauce, sugar, and half of the green onions, continue to stir-fry until the lobster is well coated and cooked through, about 5 mins ●Stir in Sichuan peppercorns, remaining butter, and sesame oil, coat evenly ●Garnish with the remaining green onions and serve immediately

Tips: ●Experiment with the amount of doubanjiang for varying levels of spiciness ●Use a well-seasoned wok for the best flavor and to prevent sticking ●Serve immediately for best taste

Nutritional Values: Calories: 309, Fat: 17g, Carbs: 5g, Protein: 30g, Sugar: 2g

CANTONESE LOBSTER WITH GARLIC AND OYSTER SAUCE

Preparation Time: 20 min

Cooking Time: 12 min

Mode of Cooking: Stir-Frying

Servings: 4

Ingredients: ●2 whole lobsters, about 1 lb each, cut into pieces ●3 Tbsp oyster sauce ●1 Tbsp soy sauce ●2 Tbsp Shaoxing wine ●4 Tbsp unsalted butter ●6 cloves garlic, minced ●2 Tbsp green onions, chopped ●1 tsp cornstarch dissolved in 2 Tbsp water ●1 Tbsp vegetable oil ●Salt and white pepper to taste ●1 Tbsp sesame oil for drizzling

Directions: ●Heat the vegetable oil and 2 Tbsp butter in a wok over medium heat until melted ●Add garlic and stir-fry until just golden, about 1 min ●Increase the heat to high, add lobster and stir-fry for about 2 mins ●Add soy sauce, oyster sauce, and Shaoxing wine, mix well ●Add the cornstarch mixture to thicken the sauce, stirring continuously for about 2 mins ●Stir in the remaining butter, green onions, and season with salt and white pepper to taste ●Drizzle with sesame oil before serving

Tips: ●Thinly slicing the garlic will enhance its flavor in the dish ●For a glossy sauce, ensure the cornstarch mixture is well-dissolved before adding ●Serve with steamed rice to enjoy the flavorful sauce

Nutritional Values: Calories: 278, Fat: 18g, Carbs: 8g, Protein: 22g, Sugar: 1g

SZECHUAN SPICY GARLIC LOBSTER

Preparation Time: 20 min
Cooking Time: 15 min
Mode of Cooking: Stir-Frying

Servings: 4

Ingredients: ●2 lb. live lobster, cut into chunks ●1 Tbsp Szechuan peppercorns ●5 cloves garlic, minced ●3 Tbsp vegetable oil ●1 Tbsp fresh ginger, minced ●2 Tbsp soy sauce ●1 Tbsp Shaoxing wine ●2 tsp sugar ●1 tsp cornstarch mixed with 1 Tbsp water ●4 green onions, chopped ●2 dried red chilies, cut into pieces

Directions: ●Place the lobster chunks in boiling water for 30 sec, then drain and pat dry ●Heat oil in a wok over medium heat, add Szechuan peppercorns and dried chilies until fragrant ●Add garlic and ginger, stir-fry for 1 min ●Increase heat to high, add lobster and stir-fry for 5-7 mins ●Add soy sauce, Shaoxing wine, and sugar, stirring well to coat ●Stir in the cornstarch mixture until the sauce thickens ●Garnish with green onions before serving

Tips: ●Use lobster shells for added flavor in the sauce if desired. ●Pat lobster dry to ensure proper stir-frying without excess moisture ●Removing seeds from chilies reduces heat if preferred

Nutritional Values: Calories: 310, Fat: 14g, Carbs: 10g, Protein: 35g, Sugar: 3g

10.2 STEAMED FISH AND SEAFOOD DIM SUM

Steamed fish and seafood dim sum represent the delicate artistry and subtle flavors that are hallmarks of refined Chinese cuisine. This cooking method, which uses gentle steam to cook food, preserves the natural flavors and textures of seafood, allowing the ingredients to speak for themselves without the interference of overpowering seasonings.

In the realm of dim sum, steamed offerings such as *har gow* (shrimp dumplings) and delicate fish rolls are not just meals; they are a showcase of culinary precision and elegance. Each piece is meticulously prepared, with wrappers so translucent you can see the pink shrimp nestled within, and fish so tender it flakes at the touch of a chopstick.

The tradition of serving steamed seafood in small, bite-sized portions allows diners to experience a variety of flavors without commitment to a single dish, making each meal a journey through the tastes and textures of the sea. It also reflects the communal aspect of Chinese dining, where sharing is part of the experience—a meal is as much about togetherness as it is about sustenance.

Steaming is not just a cooking technique but a philosophy that values health and simplicity, placing emphasis on the purity of ingredients and their inherent flavors. Engaging in the preparation of steamed seafood at home can transform your kitchen into a place of zen-like focus and creativity, where each dish is a celebration of the sea's bountiful offerings.

CANTONESE STEAMED FISH (DIU ZI YU)

Preparation Time: 20 min
Cooking Time: 12 min
Mode of Cooking: Steaming
Servings: 4

Ingredients: ●1 whole sea bass, cleaned and scaled ●2 Tbsp soy sauce ●1 Tbsp Shaoxing wine ●1 tsp sugar ●1 inch ginger, julienned ●4 scallions, sliced diagonally into 2-inch pieces ●2 Tbsp vegetable oil ●1 Tbsp sesame oil ●Cilantro leaves for garnish ●Salt to taste ●Freshly ground black pepper to taste

Directions: ●Pat the fish dry with paper towels and make 3-4 diagonal slashes on each side of the fish ●Place the fish on a heatproof plate that fits into a steamer ●Season the fish inside and out with salt and pepper ●Combine soy sauce, Shaoxing wine, and sugar in a small bowl and pour the mixture over the fish ●Top the fish with half of the ginger and scallions ●Bring water in the bottom of the steamer to a boil then carefully place the plate with the fish in the steamer ●Cover and steam over high heat for 12 minutes or until the fish is cooked through ●Heat vegetable oil and sesame oil in a small pan until smoking then pour it over the cooked fish to crisp the skin ●Garnish with remaining ginger and scallions, and cilantro leaves

Tips: ●Choose a fish with bright eyes and a fresh ocean smell for the best flavor and texture ●Serve immediately with steamed rice for a complete meal

Nutritional Values: Calories: 220, Fat: 10g, Carbs: 2g, Protein: 30g, Sugar: 1g

SOY-GINGER STEAMED SCALLOPS

Preparation Time: 15 min
Cooking Time: 10 min
Mode of Cooking: Steaming
Servings: 2

Ingredients: ●6 large sea scallops ●2 Tbsp soy sauce ●1 Tbsp mirin ●1 tsp grated ginger ●2 cloves garlic, minced ●1 scallion, finely chopped ●1 Tbsp vegetable oil ●1 tsp sesame seeds ●Lemon slices for garnish

Directions: ●Rinse scallops under cold water and pat dry ●Place scallops in a single layer on a heatproof plate that will fit into a steamer ●In a bowl, mix soy sauce, mirin, ginger, and garlic then spoon the mixture over the scallops ●Top scallops with chopped scallion ●Prepare steamer by bringing water to a boil ●Place plate with scallops in the steamer, cover, and steam for 8-10 minutes until scallops are opaque and cooked through ●Just before serving, heat vegetable oil in a small pan and then drizzle over scallops ●Sprinkle sesame seeds on top and garnish with lemon slices

Tips: ●Use fresh scallops for the best flavor and tender texture ●Do not overcook scallops to avoid them becoming tough and rubbery

Nutritional Values: Calories: 120, Fat: 5g, Carbs: 5g, Protein: 14g, Sugar: 0g

BLACK BEAN SAUCE STEAMED COD

Preparation Time: 25 min
Cooking Time: 15 min
Mode of Cooking: Steaming
Servings: 4

Ingredients: ●4 cod fillets, about 6 oz each ●2 Tbsp fermented black beans, rinsed and mashed ●2 cloves garlic, minced ●1 inch ginger, minced ●1 Tbsp soy sauce ●1 tsp sugar ●2 Tbsp Shaoxing wine ●1 Tbsp sesame oil ●4 scallions, chopped ●1 red chili, thinly sliced ●Cilantro for garnish

Directions: ●Rinse cod fillets under cold water and pat dry ●In a bowl, combine mashed black beans, garlic, ginger, soy sauce, sugar, and Shaoxing wine ●Lay cod fillets on a heatproof dish and spread the black bean mixture evenly over each fillet ●Place the dish in a preheated steamer and cover ●Steam for about 15 minutes until the fish flakes easily with a fork ●Drizzle sesame oil over the cooked fillets and garnish with scallions, red chili slices, and cilantro leaves before serving

Tips: ●Mashing the fermented black beans before using them helps to release more flavor ●Serve with jasmine rice to complement the flavors of the sauce

Nutritional Values: Calories: 200, Fat: 6g, Carbs: 4g, Protein: 34g, Sugar: 1g

10.2.2 SHRIMP DUMPLINGS (HAR GOW)

CLASSIC HAR GOW (SHRIMP DUMPLINGS)

Preparation Time: 20 min

Cooking Time: 10 min

Mode of Cooking: Steaming

Servings: 4

Ingredients: ●½ lb. shrimp, peeled and deveined ●1 Tbsp bamboo shoots, finely chopped ●1 tsp ginger, minced ●1 scallion, finely chopped ●1 Tbsp soy sauce ●1 tsp sesame oil ●1 tsp cornstarch ●1 pinch white pepper ●1 cup wheat starch ●½ cup boiling water ●1 tsp lard or vegetable shortening

Directions: ●Mix wheat starch and boiling water in a bowl until a dough forms, then knead in lard until smooth and pliable. Cover with a damp cloth and set aside ●Chop half the shrimp into chunks and the other half into a fine paste. Combine with bamboo shoots, ginger, scallion, soy sauce, sesame oil, cornstarch, and white pepper ●Roll out the dough to about 1/16 inch thick. Cut into circles using a cookie cutter ●Put a spoonful of the filling in the center of each dough circle. Pleat the edges to form the dumpling, leaving the top open ●Steam on a greased steamer for 10 min until translucent

Tips: ●Use a bamboo steamer for optimal results ●When mixing the dough, adjust boiling water as needed for a pliable texture but not sticky●Keep the dough covered at all times to prevent it from drying out

Nutritional Values: Calories: 180, Fat: 3g, Carbs: 20g, Protein: 15g, Sugar: 0g

SQUID INK SIU MAI

Preparation Time: 25 min

Cooking Time: 12 min

Mode of Cooking: Steaming

Servings: 4

Ingredients: ●½ lb. ground pork ●¼ lb. shrimp, finely chopped ●1 Tbsp squid ink ●2 Tbsp water chestnuts, finely chopped ●1 tsp soy sauce ●1 tsp Shaoxing wine ●½ tsp sesame oil ●¼ tsp ground white pepper ●1 packet wonton wrappers ●1 small carrot, finely grated for garnish

Directions: ●Combine ground pork, shrimp, squid ink, water chestnuts, soy sauce, Shaoxing wine, sesame oil, and white pepper in a bowl until well mixed ●Take a wonton wrapper and place a tbsp of filling in the center. Gather up the sides to form a cup shape, leaving the top open ●Place grated carrot on top of each dumpling for garnish ●Steam on grease-proof paper in a bamboo steamer for 12 min

Tips: ●Avoid overworking the dough to keep the dumplings tender ●Squid ink not only adds a unique flavor but also turns the dumplings a striking black color, making for an unforgettable presentation●Serve immediately while hot for best texture

Nutritional Values: Calories: 225, Fat: 8g, Carbs: 18g, Protein: 20g, Sugar: 1g

JADE DUMPLINGS

Preparation Time: 30 min

Cooking Time: 15 min

Mode of Cooking: Steaming

Servings: 4

Ingredients: ●½ lb. spinach, blanched and squeezed dry ●½ lb. shrimp, peeled and deveined ●1 Tbsp ginger, minced ●1 Tbsp cilantro, chopped ●1 tsp sesame oil ●1 tsp soy sauce ●1 pinch white pepper ●1 cup wheat starch ●½ cup tapioca starch ●¾ cup boiling water ●1 tsp vegetable oil

Directions: ●Puree the blanched spinach to a fine paste and mix with boiling water, wheat starch, tapioca starch, and vegetable oil to form a green dough. Let it rest under a damp cloth ●For the filling, chop the shrimp into a coarse paste and mix with ginger, cilantro, sesame oil, soy sauce, and white pepper ●Roll out the dough, cut into circles, and fill with the shrimp mixture before pleating into dumplings ●Steam on a lined steamer for 15 min

Tips: ●The spinach not only gives the dough its signature jade color but also adds a subtle flavor ●Keep the filling simple to let the delicate flavors shine through●Rolling the dough thinly ensures a tender, almost translucent wrapper

Nutritional Values: Calories: 200, Fat: 2g, Carbs: 32g, Protein: 14g, Sugar: 1g

Seafood soups and congee in Chinese cuisine are a symphony of flavors that bring the essence of the ocean to the table, offering a comforting warmth that nourishes both body and soul. These dishes are steeped in the tradition of transforming simple ingredients into rich, complex creations that celebrate the sea's bounty.

The delicate, nuanced flavors of seafood are ideally suited to soups and congee, where slow simmering processes meld the distinct tastes and textures of fish, shellfish, and seaweeds with aromatic broths. Dishes like *Chinese Fish Soup with Tofu and Vegetables* highlight the gentle flavors of the sea, enhanced with ginger and scallions to complement, not overwhelm, the fresh taste of the fish.

Seafood congee, meanwhile, is a heartier offering that combines rice porridge with generous servings of seafood, each spoonful delivering comfort and a subtle, briny sweetness. This dish often features scallops, shrimp, or crab, each element adding its unique flavor while absorbing the savory notes of the congee's base. It's a popular breakfast choice in coastal regions, celebrated for its simplicity and the sustained energy it provides.

Engaging in the preparation of these seafood dishes allows for an appreciation of the delicate balance required to maintain the integrity of the ingredients while enhancing their natural flavors. It's a culinary process that respects the origins of the seafood and brings forward the deep connection between the sea and Chinese culinary culture.

10.3.1 CHINESE FISH SOUP WITH TOFU AND VEGETABLES

SILVER CARP SOUP WITH PICKLED VEGETABLES AND TOFU

Preparation Time: 20 min

Cooking Time: 1 hr

Mode of Cooking: Simmering

Servings: 4

Ingredients: ●1 lb silver carp, cleaned and cut into chunks ●2 Tbsp vegetable oil ●1 large white onion, thinly sliced ●4 cloves garlic, minced ●2 inches ginger, thinly sliced ●6 cups water ●1 cup pickled mustard greens, chopped ●1 block firm tofu, cut into cubes ●1 Tbsp soy sauce ●Salt and white pepper to taste ●2 green onions, chopped for garnish

Directions: ●Heat oil in a large pot over medium heat ●Add onion, garlic, and ginger; sauté until onion is translucent ●Add the silver carp chunks; fry lightly on all sides ●Pour water into the pot; bring to a boil ●Lower the heat to a simmer; add pickled mustard greens and tofu ●Season with soy sauce, salt, and white pepper ●Cover and simmer for 1 hr, occasionally skimming any foam that forms on the surface ●Serve hot, garnished with green onions

Tips: ●Use a slotted spoon to gently remove the fish pieces if they start to fall apart during cooking to maintain the broth's clarity ●Pickled mustard greens can be adjusted based on your preference for sourness ●Adding a few drops of sesame oil before serving enhances flavor

Nutritional Values: Calories: 220, Fat: 10g, Carbs: 8g, Protein: 28g, Sugar: 3g

BRAISED SEA BASS WITH SHIITAKE MUSHROOMS AND BAMBOO SHOOTS

Preparation Time: 15 min

Cooking Time: 35 min

Mode of Cooking: Braising

Servings: 4

Ingredients: ●2 lb sea bass fillets ●2 Tbsp soy sauce ●1 Tbsp Shaoxing wine ●1 tsp sugar ●3 Tbsp vegetable oil ●8 shiitake mushrooms, rehydrated and sliced ●1 cup bamboo shoots, thinly sliced ●2 cups chicken stock ●1 star anise ●2 green onions, sliced ●1 piece of ginger, julienned ●Salt to taste

Directions: ●Marinate sea bass fillets with soy sauce, Shaoxing wine, and sugar for 10 min ●Heat oil in a skillet over medium-high heat ●Add ginger and star anise; sauté until fragrant ●Add shiitake mushrooms and bamboo shoots; sauté for 5 min ●Place the marinated sea bass on top of the mushrooms and shoots ●Pour chicken stock over the fish; bring to a boil ●Reduce heat to low, cover, and simmer for 25 min ●Uncover, increase heat to medium and cook until the sauce thickens slightly ●Season with salt ●Serve garnished with green onions

Tips: ●Sautéing mushrooms and bamboo shoots before braising adds depth to the dish's flavor ●Using a non-stick skillet prevents fish from sticking and breaking apart ●A gentle simmer keeps the fish tender

Nutritional Values: Calories: 295, Fat: 14g, Carbs: 12g, Protein: 34g, Sugar: 4g

TOFU AND SEAWEED SOUP WITH CLAMS

Preparation Time: 10 min

Cooking Time: 25 min

Mode of Cooking: Boiling

Servings: 4

Ingredients: ●2 dozen clams, cleaned ●6 cups water ●1 block soft tofu, cut into cubes ●1 cup dried seaweed, rehydrated and chopped ●2 Tbsp miso paste ●1 tsp sesame oil ●2 cloves garlic, minced ●1 tsp grated ginger ●Salt to taste ●Chopped scallions for garnish

Directions: ●In a pot, bring water to a boil ●Add clams and cook until they open, about 5-7 min ●Remove clams with a slotted spoon, discard any that did not open ●In the same water, add garlic, ginger, and rehydrated seaweed; cook for 5 min ●Lower the heat and add tofu cubes; heat through without boiling ●Dilute miso paste in a small amount of the soup water and add it back to the pot along with sesame oil ●Add the cooked clams back into the soup ●Adjust with salt ●Serve hot, garnished with scallions

Tips: ●Do not boil the soup after adding miso to preserve its flavor and beneficial properties ●Soaking dried seaweed in water prior to cooking reduces cooking time and ensures it's fully rehydrated ●Fresh clams can be substituted with canned clams, but adjust for saltiness

Nutritional Values: Calories: 180, Fat: 5g, Carbs: 10g, Protein: 25g, Sugar: 1g

10.3.2 SEAFOOD CONGEE WITH SCALLOPS AND SHRIMP

SCALLOPS AND SHRIMP SEAFOOD CONGEE

Preparation Time: 20 min

Cooking Time: 1 hr

Mode of Cooking: Simmering

Servings: 4

Ingredients: ●1 cup jasmine rice, rinsed ●6 cups chicken or vegetable broth ●1 inch ginger, thinly sliced ●¾ lb. scallops ●¾ lb. shrimp, peeled and deveined ●2 Tbsp soy sauce ●1 Tbsp sesame oil ●3 green onions, chopped ●Salt to taste ●White pepper to taste ●Fresh cilantro for garnish

Directions: ●Bring the rinsed jasmine rice and sliced ginger with 6 cups of broth to a boil in a large pot, then reduce heat to a simmer, stirring occasionally, until the rice is broken down and the congee has thickened, about 1 hr ●Season the congee with soy sauce, sesame oil, salt, and white pepper ●In the last 10 min of cooking, add the scallops and shrimp to the congee, cooking until they are just done ●Serve in bowls garnished with green onions and fresh cilantro

Tips: ●Opt for low-sodium broth to control the saltiness of the dish ●Gently stir the congee throughout cooking to prevent sticking and ensure a creamy texture ●For an extra touch, drizzle a bit more sesame oil upon serving

Nutritional Values: Calories: 320, Fat: 5g, Carbs: 38g, Protein: 27g, Sugar: 2g

GINGER LOBSTER CONGEE

Preparation Time: 30 min

Cooking Time: 1 hr 20 min

Mode of Cooking: Simmering

Servings: 4

Ingredients: ●1 cup short-grain rice, rinsed ●8 cups seafood stock ●2 Tbsp finely grated ginger ●1 lb. lobster tails, shelled and chopped ●2 Tbsp oyster sauce ●1 tsp white pepper ●2 Tbsp Shaoxing wine ●4 green onions, sliced ●1 Tbsp goji berries ●Sesame seeds for garnish

Directions: ●Combine the rinsed short-grain rice, grated ginger, and seafood stock in a large saucepan and bring to a boil. Reduce heat to low and simmer, uncovered, stirring now and then until the rice is fully broken down and congee reaches a creamy consistency, about 1 hr 20 min ●Stir in the oyster sauce, white pepper, and Shaoxing wine ●Add the lobster pieces to the pot and cook until tender, about 10 min before congee is done ●Serve hot garnished with sliced green onions, goji berries, and a sprinkle of sesame seeds

Tips: ●Lobster shells can be boiled in the stock for extra flavor before adding rice ●Goji berries add a slight sweetness and are known for their health benefits ●Shaoxing wine can be substituted with dry sherry if not available

Nutritional Values: Calories: 345, Fat: 3g, Carbs: 45g, Protein: 30g, Sugar: 3g

ABALONE MUSHROOM SEAFOOD CONGEE

Preparation Time: 25 min
Cooking Time: 1 hr 15 min
Mode of Cooking: Simmering
Servings: 4
Ingredients: ●1 cup brown rice, rinsed ●7 cups mushroom broth ●2 Tbsp ginger, minced ●200g abalone, sliced thin ●200g oyster mushrooms, roughly chopped ●2 Tbsp light soy sauce ●1 Tbsp sesame oil ●½ tsp ground white pepper ●2 spring onions, sliced ●1 red chili, thinly sliced for garnish ●Fresh coriander leaves for garnish

Directions: ●Start by boiling the brown rice with mushroom broth and minced ginger in a large pot, then lower the heat to simmer until the congee texture is thick and creamy, approximately 1 hr 15 min ●Incorporate the light soy sauce, sesame oil, and white pepper into the congee, mixing well ●Place the sliced abalone and chopped oyster mushrooms in the congee around 15 min before it finishes cooking, allowing them to cook through ●Once ready, dish the congee into bowls and embellish with spring onions, red chili slices, and coriander leaves

Tips: ●Using brown rice adds a nutty flavor and nutritious boost to the congee ●Abalone should be sliced thinly to ensure it cooks quickly and evenly ●Chilis can be adjusted based on preferred spice levels

Nutritional Values: Calories: 260, Fat: 4g, Carbs: 43g, Protein: 18g, Sugar: 3g

CHAPTER 11: SWEET ENDINGS

11.1 TRADITIONAL CHINESE DESSERTS

Traditional Chinese desserts, often characterized by their subtlety and elegance, offer a gentle close to the vibrant flavors of a Chinese meal. These desserts do not overpower but rather soothe the palate with their delicate sweetness and often, nutritional benefits, rooted in China's deep herbal lore.

One of the most cherished classics is the *Red Bean Paste Bun*, known for its smooth, sweet filling encased in a fluffy dough. This dessert is not just a treat; it's a symbol of luck and prosperity. Equally revered are *Egg Custard Tarts*, which marry a creamy, delicate custard with a flaky pastry—a legacy of Portuguese influence in southern China, adapted into local tastes and ingredients.

These desserts often incorporate ingredients like lotus seeds, red beans, and dates, which are believed to offer more than just flavor—they are thought to impart balance and health to the body. The preparation of these sweets is as much about creating harmony within as it is about crafting flavors that delight.

Exploring traditional Chinese desserts allows one to delve into a world where every ingredient is chosen for its meaning and every recipe tells a story. This journey through China's dessert repertoire is not just an indulgence in sweet treats; it's an embrace of centuries-old traditions that celebrate the refined and the understated in culinary art.

11.1.1 RED BEAN PASTE BUNS (DOU SHA BAO)

RED BEAN PASTE BUNS (DOU SHA BAO)

Preparation Time: 30 min.
Cooking Time: 20 min.
Mode of Cooking: Steaming
Servings: 12
Ingredients: ●2 cups all-purpose flour ●1 Tbsp sugar ●1/2 tsp salt ●1 Tbsp instant yeast ●3/4 cup warm water ●1 Tbsp vegetable oil ●1 cup red bean paste
Directions: ●Mix flour, sugar, salt, and instant yeast in a large bowl ●Gradually add warm water and vegetable oil, stirring until a soft dough forms ●Knead the dough on a lightly floured surface until smooth, about 10 min. ●Place the dough in a greased bowl, cover with a damp cloth, and let it rise in a warm place until doubled in size, about 1 hr. ●Punch down the dough, then divide into 12 equal pieces ●Flatten each piece into a circle, then spoon about 1 Tbsp of red bean paste into the center ●Gather the edges to enclose the filling and pinch to seal ●Place each bun on a small piece of parchment paper ●Let the buns rest for 10 min. ●Steam the buns over boiling water for 20 min. until puffy and cooked through

Tips: ●Ensure the water is simmering gently to prevent water from splashing onto the buns ●Brush the buns with a little vegetable oil after steaming for a glossy finish ●If red bean paste is too thick, mix with a small amount of water to make it easier to work with
Nutritional Values: Calories: 180, Fat: 2g, Carbs: 34g, Protein: 4g, Sugar: 10g

BLACK SESAME SEED BUNS

Preparation Time: 35 min.
Cooking Time: 25 min.
Mode of Cooking: Steaming

Servings: 12

Ingredients: ●2 cups all-purpose flour ●2 Tbsp black sesame seeds ●1 Tbsp sugar ●1/2 tsp salt ●1 Tbsp instant yeast ●1 cup warm water ●1 Tbsp sesame oil ●1 cup black sesame seed paste

Directions: ●In a dry pan, lightly toast black sesame seeds until fragrant, then grind them to a powder ●Combine flour, ground black sesame seeds, sugar, salt, and yeast in a bowl ●Add warm water and sesame oil, mixing to form a soft dough ●Knead on a floured surface until elastic, about 15 min. ●Allow to rise in a greased, covered bowl until doubled, about 1 hr. ●Punch down dough, then divide and shape into 12 balls ●Flatten each ball and fill with 1 Tbsp black sesame seed paste, sealing edges firmly ●Place on parchment paper squares and let rise for 15 min. ●Steam over boiling water for 25 min. until expanded and set

Tips: ●Use a cloth to cover the lid of the steamer to absorb condensation ●Serve with a sprinkle of toasted sesame seeds on top for extra texture ●Store in an airtight container to keep them soft

Nutritional Values: Calories: 220, Fat: 6g, Carbs: 36g, Protein: 5g, Sugar: 12g

LOTUS SEED PASTE BUNS

Preparation Time: 40 min.
Cooking Time: 20 min.
Mode of Cooking: Steaming
Servings: 12

Ingredients: ●2 cups all-purpose flour ●1 Tbsp sugar ●1/2 tsp salt ●1 Tbsp instant yeast ●3/4 cup warm water ●1 Tbsp vegetable oil ●1 cup lotus seed paste

Directions: ●Combine flour, sugar, salt, and yeast in a mixing bowl ●Add warm water and oil, mixing until a dough forms ●Knead on a floured surface until smooth, about 10 min. ●Let rise in an oiled bowl, covered, until doubled, about 1 hr. ●Divide dough into 12 pieces, roll each out, and place 1 Tbsp lotus seed paste in the center ●Enclose the filling by pinching edges together ●Put each bun on parchment paper ●Allow to rest for 10 min before steaming over boiling water for 20 min.

Tips: ●For an added touch, shape the buns like lotus flowers before steaming ●Apply a thin layer of oil to

the buns for a shiny surface after steaming ●Lotus seed paste can be made or purchased pre-made for convenience

Nutritional Values: Calories: 190, Fat: 3g, Carbs: 35g, Protein: 5g, Sugar: 11g

11.1.2 EGG CUSTARD TARTS (DAN TAT)

BLACK SESAME EGG CUSTARD TARTS

Preparation Time: 20 min.
Cooking Time: 25 min.
Mode of Cooking: Baking
Servings: 12

Ingredients: ●For the Custard: 4 large eggs ●1 cup whole milk ●½ cup heavy cream ●⅓ cup sugar ●2 Tbsp black sesame seeds, toasted and ground ●1 tsp vanilla extract ●For the Pastry: 1½ cups all-purpose flour ●¼ cup sugar ●½ cup unsalted butter, cold and diced ●1 large egg yolk ●2 Tbsp ice water

Directions: ●Prepare the Pastry: Combine flour and sugar in a food processor; pulse to mix ●Add butter and pulse until mixture resembles coarse crumbs ●Add egg yolk and ice water; pulse until dough forms ●Wrap in plastic; chill for 30 min. ●Roll out dough and cut into 12 rounds; press into tart pans ●Prepare the Custard: Whisk together eggs, milk, cream, sugar, ground black sesame seeds, and vanilla until smooth ●Strain mixture to remove any lumps ●Preheat oven to 375°F (190°C) ●Pour custard into tart shells ●Bake for 20-25 min., or until custard is set ●Cool before serving

Tips: ●Use a fine sieve to ensure a smooth custard ●Toast sesame seeds lightly to enhance flavor ●Chill tarts in the refrigerator for refreshing contrast

Nutritional Values: Calories: 230, Fat: 14g, Carbs: 22g, Protein: 5g, Sugar: 9g

GINGER HONEY EGG CUSTARD TARTS

Preparation Time: 25 min.
Cooking Time: 30 min.
Mode of Cooking: Baking
Servings: 12

Ingredients: ●For the Custard: 4 large eggs ●1 cup whole milk ●½ cup cream ●½ cup honey ●1 Tbsp fresh ginger, grated ●For the Pastry: 1½ cups all-purpose flour •¼ cup confectioners' sugar •½ cup unsalted butter, cold and cubed •1 large egg yolk •3 Tbsp cold water

Directions: •Prepare the Pastry: In a bowl, mix flour and confectioners' sugar •Rub in butter until mixture is crumbly •Stir in egg yolk and water to form a dough; chill for 30 min. •Roll out and fit into tart pans •Prepare the Custard: Beat eggs, milk, cream, honey, and ginger until well combined •Preheat oven to 350°F (175°C) •Pour into pastry cases •Bake for 30 min., or until set •Allow to cool before serving

Tips: •Infuse ginger in milk and cream by heating gently then cooling for a stronger flavor •Use local honey for better taste and benefits •Serve with a sprinkle of powdered ginger for extra zing

Nutritional Values: Calories: 270, Fat: 16g, Carbs: 28g, Protein: 4g, Sugar: 16g

JASMINE TEA EGG CUSTARD TARTS

Preparation Time: 15 min.
Cooking Time: 20 min.
Mode of Cooking: Baking
Servings: 12

Ingredients: •For the Custard: 3 large eggs •1 cup whole milk •½ cup cream •⅓ cup sugar •2 Tbsp jasmine tea leaves •For the Pastry: 2 cups pastry flour •⅓ cup sugar •⅔ cup unsalted butter, chilled and diced •1 large egg •1 Tbsp cold water

Directions: •Prepare the Pastry: Sift flour and sugar together •Work in butter until mixture resembles fine breadcrumbs •Mix in egg and water to form a dough; chill for an hour •Press into tart molds •Prepare the Custard: Heat milk and cream with jasmine tea leaves until just simmering; remove from heat and let steep for 10 min. •Strain and mix with eggs and sugar •Preheat oven to 325°F (163°C) •Fill tart shells with custard mixture •Bake for 20 min. or until custard has set •Cool before serving

Tips: •Steep tea leaves longer for a stronger flavor •Serve with jasmine tea for a themed dessert pairing •Dust with powdered sugar for a sweet finish

Nutritional Values: Calories: 250, Fat: 15g, Carbs: 24g, Protein: 4g, Sugar: 10g

11.2 FRUIT-BASED SWEETS AND TREATS

In Chinese cuisine, the natural sweetness and refreshing qualities of fruits are often harnessed to create desserts that delight both the eye and the palate. Fruit-based sweets and treats are a vibrant category, offering a lighter, healthier alternative to more decadent desserts, and they beautifully showcase the seasonal bounty of the region.

One such beloved treat is the *Mango Pudding*, a smooth, creamy dessert that captures the essence of mangoes at their peak. Its bright flavor and silky texture make it a favorite ending to meals, particularly in the warmer months. Another popular choice is *Coconut Sticky Rice with Mango*, a dish that combines the tropical richness of coconut with the sweet, juicy slices of fresh mango atop glutinous rice—a delightful contrast of flavors and textures.

These desserts are often appreciated not just for their taste but for their aesthetic appeal. They are typically presented with a flourish, garnished with fresh fruits and often a drizzle of sweet syrup, making them as beautiful as they are delicious. The simplicity of these dishes belies the careful attention to balance and proportion, ensuring that the natural flavors of the fruits shine through.

Preparing these fruit-based desserts offers a joyful exploration into the lighter side of Chinese sweet treats, providing a refreshing finale to any meal and a nod to the country's vast, diverse climate and flora. Each bite is a celebration of nature's generosity, transformed through the culinary traditions that honor freshness and simplicity.

11.2.1 MANGO PUDDING

LYCHEE AND MANGO PUDDING

Preparation Time: 15 min

Cooking Time: 4 hrs chilling
Mode of Cooking: No Cooking

Servings: 6

Ingredients: •2 cups fresh mango, pureed •1 cup canned lychee, drained and chopped •3 Tbsp gelatin powder •1/2 cup hot water •1 cup cold water •1/2 cup sugar •1 cup coconut milk

Directions: •Dissolve gelatin powder in hot water then add cold water •In a separate bowl, combine mango puree, lychee, sugar, and coconut milk, stirring until sugar dissolves •Mix in the gelatin solution until well combined •Pour into moulds or a serving dish and refrigerate for at least 4 hours until set

Tips: •Serve with extra lychee or mango slices for garnish •Can be made a day ahead for enhanced flavor•Use ripe mangoes for a sweeter taste

Nutritional Values: Calories: 220, Fat: 7g, Carbs: 38g, Protein: 3g, Sugar: 35g

DRAGON FRUIT AND PINEAPPLE GELATO

Preparation Time: 30 min

Cooking Time: 5 hrs freezing

Mode of Cooking: No Cooking

Servings: 4

Ingredients: •1 large dragon fruit, peeled and cubed •1 cup fresh pineapple, cubed •1/2 cup sugar •2 Tbsp lime juice •1 tsp lime zest •1 cup heavy cream

Directions: •Puree dragon fruit and pineapple in a blender until smooth •Mix in sugar, lime juice, and zest until sugar dissolves •Whip the heavy cream to soft peaks and gently fold into the fruit mixture •Pour into a loaf pan and freeze for at least 5 hours, stirring every 30 minutes for the first 2 hours

Tips: •Use a fork to scrape the surface to create a fluffy texture •Serve immediately for best texture•Garnish with lime zest or mint leaves for an added zing

Nutritional Values: Calories: 350, Fat: 22g, Carbs: 36g, Protein: 2g, Sugar: 34g

CHILLED KUMQUAT AND HONEY SOUP

Preparation Time: 20 min

Cooking Time: 2 hrs chilling

Mode of Cooking: No Cooking

Servings: 4

Ingredients: •2 cups kumquats, halved and deseeded •1/4 cup local honey •3 cups water •1 stick cinnamon •1 star anise •1 Tbsp fresh ginger, minced

Directions: •Combine water, honey, cinnamon stick, star anise, and ginger in a saucepan and simmer for 10 minutes •Let cool then strain over the halved kumquats •Refrigerate for at least 2 hours to infuse flavors

Tips: •Serve chilled as a refreshing soup or dessert •Can add a splash of sparkling water before serving for a fizzy twist•Garnish with mint leaves or a drizzle of extra honey

Nutritional Values: Calories: 140, Fat: 0g, Carbs: 36g, Protein: 1g, Sugar: 33g

11.2.2 COCONUT STICKY RICE WITH MANGO

MANGO AND COCONUT JELLY SQUARES

Preparation Time: 15 min.

Cooking Time: 4 hrs. Refrigeration time

Mode of Cooking: No Cooking

Servings: 8

Ingredients: •1 large ripe mango, puréed •400 ml canned coconut milk •2 Tbsp agar agar powder •½ cup warm water •⅓ cup granulated sugar •1 tsp vanilla extract •Pinch of salt •Fresh mango cubes for garnish •Mint leaves for garnish

Directions: •Dissolve agar agar in warm water and let it sit for 5 min •In a saucepan, combine coconut milk, sugar, vanilla extract, and salt, then bring to a simmer over medium heat, stirring until sugar dissolves •Add dissolved agar to the saucepan and whisk for 2 min. over low heat •Remove from heat and cool for about 10 min. •Stir in mango purée •Pour mixture into a square dish and refrigerate until set, about 4 hrs. •Cut into squares and garnish with fresh mango cubes and mint leaves before serving

Tips: •Use ripe mangoes for a sweeter flavor •If the jelly doesn't set, check if the agar agar was completely dissolved in water •Serve chilled for the best texture

Nutritional Values: Calories: 150, Fat: 8g, Carbs: 18g, Protein: 2g, Sugar: 15g

TROPICAL MANGO COCONUT ICE CREAM

Preparation Time: 30 min.

Cooking Time: 4 hrs. Freezing time

Mode of Cooking: No Cooking

Servings: 6

Ingredients: •2 ripe mangoes, peeled and cubed •1 can (14 oz.) full-fat coconut milk •¼ cup honey or to taste •Juice of 1 lime •1 tsp vanilla extract •Pinch of salt •Toasted coconut flakes for serving

Directions: •Place mango cubes in a blender and purée until smooth •Add coconut milk, honey, lime juice, vanilla extract, and salt to the blender, and pulse until well combined •Pour the mixture into an ice cream maker and churn according to manufacturer's instructions, usually about 20-25 min. •Transfer to a freezer-safe container and freeze until firm, about 4 hrs. •Serve with toasted coconut flakes sprinkled on top

Tips: •Use cold coconut milk for a smoother ice cream texture •Freeze the ice cream container beforehand to prevent ice crystals from forming •Adjust honey according to the sweetness of the mangoes

Nutritional Values: Calories: 280, Fat: 20g, Carbs: 26g, Protein: 2g, Sugar: 22g

Preparation Time: 35 min.
Cooking Time: 25 min.
Mode of Cooking: Stove Top
Servings: 4

Ingredients: •1 cup jasmine rice, rinsed •1 ripe mango, cut into bite-sized pieces •1 can (14 oz.) coconut milk •2 cups water •½ cup sugar •½ tsp salt •1 cinnamon stick •Zest of 1 lime •¼ cup toasted coconut flakes for garnish •Mint leaves for garnish

Directions: •In a medium saucepan, bring water, coconut milk, sugar, salt, and cinnamon stick to a boil over medium heat •Add rice and reduce heat to low •Simmer uncovered, stirring occasionally, until rice is tender and mixture thickens, about 20-25 min. •Remove from heat and discard the cinnamon stick •Stir in lime zest and let cool for a few minutes •Fold in mango pieces •Serve warm or chilled, garnished with toasted coconut flakes and mint leaves

Tips: •Use canned coconut milk for a creamier texture •Pair with a dry Riesling to complement the dish's sweetness •For extra richness, blend a portion of the pudding before adding mango

Nutritional Values: Calories: 420, Fat: 18g, Carbs: 60g, Protein: 5g, Sugar: 30g

11.3 MODERN TWISTS ON CLASSIC DESSERTS

In the realm of Chinese desserts, the fusion of tradition with modern innovation has given rise to an exciting array of sweets that marry the old with the new. This sub-chapter explores how classic desserts have been reimagined to suit contemporary tastes, presenting a delicious blend of heritage and creativity.

Take, for instance, the *Green Tea Matcha Ice Cream*, which infuses the ancient, earthy tones of matcha into the creamy delight of ice cream, creating a dessert that is both refreshing and rich with the depth of traditional tea culture. Similarly, *Black Sesame Seed Balls*, traditionally enjoyed during festivals, are being reenvisioned. These days, they might be filled with chocolate or even espresso fillings, offering a new twist on the nutty, comforting flavors of black sesame. These modern adaptations do not just cater to changing palates but also celebrate the versatility of Chinese culinary traditions. They bridge generations, linking the past with the present through flavors that resonate with both memory and innovation. By incorporating new ingredients and techniques, these desserts expand the boundaries of what is traditionally expected, while still paying homage to the culinary foundations laid by centuries of Chinese cooks.

Creating these modern twists provides an adventurous culinary challenge that encourages experimentation and personal expression in the kitchen, making each dish a testament to both the enduring legacy and the evolving nature of Chinese cuisine.

MATCHA MOCHI ICE CREAM

Preparation Time: 40 min

Cooking Time: 4 hrs (Freezing Time)

Mode of Cooking: No Bake, Freezing

Servings: 12

Ingredients: ●1 cup glutinous rice flour ●1/4 cup white sugar ●1 Tbsp matcha green tea powder ●3/4 cup water ●1 cup premium vanilla ice cream, softened ●Cornstarch for dusting

Directions: ●Combine glutinous rice flour, sugar, and matcha powder in a bowl, mixing well ●Gradually add water, stirring until smooth ●Strain mixture into a microwave-safe bowl ●Cover with plastic wrap and microwave on high for 2 min, then stir ●Microwave again for 1 more min or until mixture becomes translucent ●Dust a work surface with cornstarch ●Turn out the dough onto the surface and allow to cool slightly ●Roll the dough into a thin layer and cut out circles with a cookie cutter ●Place a small scoop of vanilla ice cream on each dough circle ●Encase the ice cream with the mochi dough, seal, and place them seam-side down on a tray ●Freeze until firm

Tips: ●Dust hands and work surface with cornstarch to prevent sticking ●Work quickly to prevent the ice cream from melting ●If the dough becomes too sticky, freeze briefly for easier handling

Nutritional Values: Calories: 100, Fat: 2g, Carbs: 18g, Protein: 1g, Sugar: 10g

SESAME MATCHA ICE CREAM WITH HONEY SWIRL

Preparation Time: 15 min

Cooking Time: 6 hrs (Freezing Time)

Mode of Cooking: No Churn

Servings: 8

Ingredients: ●2 cups heavy cream ●1 can (14 oz) sweetened condensed milk ●2 Tbsp matcha green tea powder ●1/4 cup toasted sesame seeds ●1/4 cup honey

Directions: ●Whip the heavy cream until stiff peaks form ●In another bowl, combine sweetened condensed milk with matcha powder and mix thoroughly ●Gently fold the whipped cream into the matcha mixture to keep it airy ●Fold in toasted sesame seeds ●Pour half of the mixture into a loaf pan ●Drizzle half of the honey over the mixture ●Pour in the remaining mixture and top with the rest of the honey ●Use a knife to swirl the honey through the ice cream ●Freeze until solid

Tips: ●Toast sesame seeds in a dry pan over medium heat until fragrant for added depth ●Use high-quality matcha for the best flavor ●For a firmer texture, freeze overnight

Nutritional Values: Calories: 348, Fat: 22g, Carbs: 32g, Protein: 5g, Sugar: 30g

DRAGON FRUIT AND MATCHA ICE CREAM BARS

Preparation Time: 30 min

Cooking Time: 5 hrs (Freezing Time)

Mode of Cooking: No Bake, Freezing

Servings: 10 Bars

Ingredients: ●1 large dragon fruit, peeled and cubed ●2 cups Greek yogurt ●3 Tbsp matcha powder ●1/4 cup honey ●1/2 cup crushed pistachios for garnish

Directions: ●Blend dragon fruit until smooth ●In a large bowl, mix Greek yogurt, matcha powder, and honey until well combined ●Fold in the pureed dragon fruit until the mixture is uniformly colored ●Pour the mixture into an ice cream bar mold ●Sprinkle crushed pistachios on top of each bar ●Insert sticks and freeze until solid

Tips: ●For a vegan option, substitute Greek yogurt with coconut yogurt ●If the mixture is too thick to pour, gently thin with a little milk or plant-based milk ●Run the molds under warm water for a few seconds to easily release the bars

Nutritional Values: Calories: 165, Fat: 4g, Carbs: 25g, Protein: 10g, Sugar: 19g

11.3.2 BLACK SESAME SEED BALLS (JIAN DUI)

MATCHA AND BLACK SESAME SEED BALLS

Preparation Time: 20 min

Cooking Time: 15 min

Mode of Cooking: Frying

Servings: 25

Ingredients: ●1 cup sweet rice flour ●¼ cup caster sugar ●½ cup water ●2 Tbsp matcha powder ●½ cup black sesame seeds, toasted ●¼ cup peanut butter ●Oil for frying ●1 Tbsp honey

Directions: ●Combine sweet rice flour, caster sugar, matcha powder, and water in a bowl and mix until a smooth dough forms ●Divide the dough into small pieces and roll each into a ball ●Mix toasted black sesame seeds with peanut butter and honey in a separate bowl to form the filling ●Flatten each dough ball and place a small amount of filling in the center, then wrap the dough around the filling and roll back into a ball ●Heat oil in a deep fryer or deep pan to 350°F (175°C) ●Fry the balls in batches, turning occasionally, until golden brown and cooked through, about 3 to 4 minutes ●Drain on paper towels

Tips: ●Do not overfill the sesame balls as they might burst during frying ●To achieve a uniform green hue, ensure the matcha powder is finely sieved before usage ●Adjust the sweetness of the filling according to taste

Nutritional Values: Calories: 100, Fat: 5g, Carbs: 12g, Protein: 2g, Sugar: 5g

CHOCOLATE-COATED BLACK SESAME SEED BALLS

Preparation Time: 30 min
Cooking Time: 10 min
Mode of Cooking: Chilling
Servings: 15
Ingredients: ●1 cup black sesame seeds ●½ cup fine sugar ●1 cup mochi flour ●¾ cup water ●1 tsp vanilla extract ●200g dark chocolate, melted ●White sesame seeds for coating

Directions: ●Toast black sesame seeds until fragrant, then grind with sugar until fine ●Mix mochi flour and water in a saucepan over medium heat, stirring until a thick paste forms ●Remove from heat, add vanilla extract and black sesame mixture, and knead until smooth ●Form the dough into small balls and chill until firm, about 20 minutes ●Dip each ball into melted dark chocolate and immediately roll in white sesame seeds to coat ●Place on a parchment-lined tray and chill until the chocolate sets

Tips: ●Use high-quality dark chocolate for a rich taste and glossy finish ●Keep the balls chilled prior to dipping in chocolate to prevent melting ●If dough is too sticky, dust your hands with mochi flour when rolling

Nutritional Values: Calories: 120, Fat: 7g, Carbs: 13g, Protein: 3g, Sugar: 8g

CRANBERRY AND BLACK SESAME BRITTLE

Preparation Time: 15 min
Cooking Time: 20 min
Mode of Cooking: Baking
Servings: 10
Ingredients: ●1 cup granulated sugar ●3 Tbsp water ●3 Tbsp light corn syrup ●½ cup dried cranberries ●½ cup black sesame seeds ●1 tsp butter ●¼ tsp baking soda

Directions: ●Preheat oven to 350°F (175°C) ●Line a baking sheet with parchment paper ●In a heavy saucepan, combine sugar, water, and corn syrup and cook over medium heat, stirring until sugar dissolves ●Increase heat and bring to a boil without stirring until mixture turns a golden color, about 10 minutes ●Remove from heat and quickly stir in butter, baking soda, dried cranberries, and black sesame seeds ●Pour immediately onto the prepared baking sheet and spread into a thin layer with a spatula ●Bake in the preheated oven until bubbly and slightly darker, about 10 minutes ●Cool completely before breaking into pieces

Tips: ●Work quickly after adding baking soda to avoid the mixture hardening in the pan ●For a twist, sprinkle a pinch of sea salt over the brittle before baking for a sweet and salty taste ●Ensure the brittle is spread thinly for a perfect snap

Nutritional Values: Calories: 180, Fat: 4g, Carbs: 34g, Protein: 2g, Sugar: 28g

DOWNLOAD YOUR BONUS

Chinese Herbal Medicine and Cuisine

Dear reader,

thank you very much for showing interest in my book. I hope it was to your liking, I invite you to let me know what you thought of it via a review on amazon

with love

Chu Hua

Made in the USA
Coppell, TX
01 December 2024

41413126R10059